# CONTENTS

# Why, God?

## Learning to Understand the Ways of Our Creator

by

### John I. "Skip" Blythe

Published by:

*Oak of Acadiana Publications*
18896 Greenwell Springs RD
Greenwell Springs, LA 70739
www.thepublishedword.com

Oak of Acadiana Publications is a publishing imprint of McDougal & Associates, an organization dedicated to the spreading the Gospel of the Lord Jesus Christ to as many people as possible in the shortest time possible.

ISBN 13: 978-1-934769-29-4

Printed in the United States of America
For worldwide distribution

# Why, God?

Oak of Acadiana Publications
18896 Greenwell Springs RD
Greenwell Springs, LA 70739
www.thepublishedword.com

# INTRODUCTION

How many times have you heard asked (or asked yourself) the question "Why, God?" For instance, we ask:

- Why did You allow my loved one to die before their time?
- Why did You allow me to go through that divorce?
- Why did You allow me to lose my house, my car, my family, my job, my child, a brother, a sister or a pet?

You may have also heard asked or asked yourself this type of question: "Why, God, did You not intervene in this or that situation?" Most of us have done it at one time or another, and many of us do it often. At the very least, this would seem to indicate that we acknowledge the existence of God, and that's a good thing!

But God may sometimes be asking us some questions too: "Did you ask Me why I did or didn't answer your prayers?" or "Did you thank Me when I did or didn't answer your prayers?" It's very normal for us to ask God questions, for this is a form of communication with Him.

But it's also important that we be still long enough to listen for His answers.

Have you ever heard from God? Sometimes He speaks to us with a still, small voice. Sometimes He speaks through the Word of God, the Bible. One thing that He always says when He speaks and something that He has always said through the ages is, "I love you."

Did you know that God loves you? The Bible assures us that He does. John 3:16 declares:

*For God so loved the world that He gave His only begotten Son, that whoever believes in Him should not perish but have everlasting life.*

We'll discuss this fact of God's love for you more in a later chapter of the book. God not only loves, but He *is* love. The Bible says:

*God is love; and he that lives in love lives in God, and God in him.*                                   1 John 4:16

Let's establish an important principle right here at the start. **Because God is love, everything He does or does not do in the earth and in each of our lives is motivated by that love.** This is one the most important truths you will find in this book. Why do I say that? Since God is love, then, everything He does is done because of His love for you, and everything He allows to happen is allowed to happen because of His love for you. That gets us back to some of our questions to God.

**8**

- God, why did You allow this in my life?
- God, why is there poverty in the world?
- God, why do You allow wars and famine and injustice and sadness and loneliness and hurt and pain?
- If You are love, then why do You allow bad things to happen?

Have you ever asked any of these questions or heard others ask them? I'm almost sure you have, and I trust that what we learn in this book will answer some of those important questions for you.

*John I. "Skip" Blythe*
*Greenwell Springs, Louisiana*

# CHAPTER 1

# WHY GOD DOES WHAT HE DOES

*So God created man in his own image, in the image of God created he him; male and female created he them.*

Genesis 1:27

Way back in the Garden of Eden, when Adam and Eve were created by God, that creation was performed to perfection. In that newly created world, there was no sin, no pain, no sickness, and no death. Everything was beautiful, and everything was pure. And that included man.

Adam and Eve had daily communication and fellowship with God. He told them that they could eat of any tree in the garden—except for one, and that particular tree was called *"the tree of the knowledge of good and evil"* (Genesis 2:17).

Well, you know the story ...

## The Entrance of Sin into a Perfect World

Eve was tempted by the serpent, whom we now know as "Satan," to eat of the one tree that God said they should *not* eat of. Satan told Eve that when she ate of that forbidden fruit her eyes would be opened, and she and Adam would become *"like God," "knowing"* the difference between *"good and evil"* (Genesis 3:5). Satan was tempting Eve with the sin of pride, the same sin that got him cast out of Heaven to Earth.

God had told Adam and Eve not to eat of that one tree because, if they did, they would die. But now the serpent contradicted that statement, telling Eve, *"You will not surely die"* (Genesis 3:4). He was correct in one aspect; Adam and Eve would not die physically (at that time), but they certainly would die spiritually. Their pure relationship with God was ended that day because of their disobedience to Him.

It was at this point, with the disobedience of Adam and Eve, in eating the forbidden fruit, that sin entered into the world. And, because of their sin, they were now cast out of the garden and, thus, lost the sweet fellowship and communion with God they had enjoyed until that moment.

## Is There No Hope?

**Sin always separates us from God.** Have you ever noticed that when you sin, you no longer want to talk to Him? The Bible says, in Romans 5:12:

**12**

*Therefore, just as through one man [Adam] sin entered the world, and death through sin, and thus death spread to all men, because all sinned.*

You might say, "Wow, it sounds like there's no hope for humanity or for me." But there is hope, my friend. The Son of God, Jesus Christ, made a way for us to return to the good graces of the Father. We will discuss how this is to be done later in the book.

## OUR CREATOR ENDOWED US WITH FREE WILL

Again, God told Adam and Eve that they could eat of any tree in the garden—except for that one. They had all they needed and could have had a wonderful life, but they chose to disobey God and to sin. What does this mean? Adam and Eve made a *choice*, and God gives all of us choices too. He has endowed each of us with what is called "free will." This means that He doesn't force us to do anything. We can choose what to do or not to do in any given situation. Unfortunately, because we are frail human beings, our choices are not always the right ones. They are often sinful, and they cause pain—for us and for others.

God's desire is for us to make right choices in life, and He is willing to help us know what those right choices should be. This requires that we know Him and His ways so well that, when we are confronted with any variety of choices, we will know which ones are right and which ones are wrong—because we know Him.

Even though the wrong choices we make cause pain and misery in our lives and in the lives of others, God must allow us to make these choices—even when He knows that we will not or have not chosen the very best in life. Again, His will is that we make good choices, those that will not harm ourselves or others. He wants us to respect the rights of others, as He expects them to respect our rights. This requires that we be more like Him.

## WE ARE MADE IN HIS IMAGE

The truth is that we were made in God's image (see Genesis 1:27). What does this mean? To be made in the image of God is to look like Him, not to be Him. So what does God look like? No one has ever seen His face, but we know what His character is. He is love. So, what does the Bible say about love?

One description of love is found in the New Testament in 1 Corinthians 13. It says this:

*Love suffers long and is kind; love does not envy; love does not parade itself, is not puffed up; does not behave rudely, does not seek its own, is not provoked, thinks no evil; does not rejoice in iniquity, but rejoices in the truth; bears all things, believes all things, hopes all things, endures all things. Love never fails.*

1 Corinthians 13:4-8

God's highest will is that we exhibit His main character trait (love) in everything that we do. If we could live our lives motivated by love for others, we would have a lot less problems, and we would cause a lot less pain.

Again, because God is love, everything that He does is motivated by love. This is true even when bad things seem to happen to us. Sometimes He allows things to come to our lives that seem hard to us, but He has allowed them because He knows that bearing these things, whatever they happen to be, will make us more like Him. This simple truth explains a lot about what God does, and it answers many of our nagging questions.

## GOD IS OFTEN OPPOSITE OF US

Now, let's look at some of the ways God does things opposite than we would, if we were Him, remembering that He does it all to show us His love.

Have you ever noticed that what God does doesn't always seem to make sense to us? He doesn't always do things the way we would, or in the way we think He should. And when this is true, who do you suppose is right, the almighty Creator of all things or us? When writing to the Romans, Paul spoke of a *"potter"*:

*Does not the potter have power over the clay, from the same lump to make one vessel for honor and another for dishonor?*                    Romans 9:21

That *"potter,"* of course, is God. Here Paul indicates that God, as the Master Potter, has power over the clay to form it in any way He chooses. A potter may create one vessel to hold flowers and another to hold water. It's up to Him. In context, the passage goes like this:

*O man, who are you to reply against God? Will the thing formed say to him who formed it, "Why have you made me like this?" Does not the potter have power over the clay, from the same lump to make one vessel for honor and another for dishonor?*

Romans 9:19-21

In other words, God knows what's best for us, and that's the reason He often guides our lives in ways that are opposite from the way we think He should. We must trust Him and learn to rest in His will.

The Bible is full of true-life stories about real people in different generations who didn't understand the ways of God and thought they would rather handle their lives in their own ways. It's also full of stories about men and women whom you and I wouldn't think God would or could ever use. Let's explore some of those stories to discover more about how God, our Creator, thinks, so that we can understand His ways and the answers to our common question, *Why, God?*.

Why, God?

# CHAPTER 2

# WHY A JUST MAN SUFFERED

*There was a man in the land of Uz, whose name was Job; and that man was blameless and upright, and one who feared God and shunned evil.* Job 1:1

One of the most difficult cases to understand in the Old Testament is the case of Job. The Bible calls him *"perfect and upright"* (KJV) and says that he *"feared God and departed from evil."* This being the case, he should have been a very blessed man.

## JOB WAS BLESSED, BUT ...

Job *was* blessed. He was blessed with a wife, seven sons, and three daughters. He was very prosperous, so prosperous that he was said to be *"the greatest of all the people of the East"* (Job 1:3). Then, one day, a very strange scene played out in Heaven, a scene that would spell the end of much of Job's material blessings. And, today, thousands of years later, Bible scholars are still trying to decide what exactly happened to Job and why.

# A STRANGE MEETING IN HEAVEN

The Bible describes a meeting that took place in Heaven. It says that the meeting was attended by *"the sons of God,"* and that, for some odd reason, Satan came too (Job 1:6). When God asked Satan what he was doing there, he answered simply that he had come from going to and fro in the earth and from walking up and down in it (same verse).

God immediately took this opportunity to bring up the subject of His servant Job:

> *Then the* LORD *said to Satan, "Have you considered My servant Job, that there is none like him on the earth, a blameless and upright man, one who fears God and shuns evil?"*  Job 1:8

Satan answered God that Job only served Him because He had put a hedge of protection around him, his house, and his possessions. He said further that God had blessed the work of Job's hands, and his substance had greatly increased in the land. If that blessing were removed for a time, Satan insinuated (in no uncertain terms), if God were to put forth His hand and touch all that Job had, the man would turn on Him and curse Him to his face. What Satan was describing seems clearly to have been a test of sorts, a severe one, but only a test nevertheless.

## GOD APPROVES THE TEST

So, what did God do? He actually gave Satan permission to attack all that Job had. The only limitation he placed on the activities of the adversary was that he spare Job's life. This has to mean that tests are okay with God, even severe ones. He trusts His children to be faithful to Him whatever comes their way, and He has the right to test them in any way He sees fit.

Suddenly, without warning, enemy invaders attacked Job's herds, stealing the animals and killing the servants who tended them. Fire fell from Heaven and burned his sheep to death, likewise killing the servants who kept them. Then, a great wind from the wilderness destroyed the house where his sons and daughters were having a feast, and they were all killed. Wow! All of that in such short order!

What would your response have been if something so tragic had happened to you? The Bible says that Job did something very amazing:

*Then Job arose, tore his robe, and shaved his head; and he fell to the ground and worshiped.*          Job 1:20

Wow! What a response! This man really loved God.

Job went on to speak words just as amazing as his deeds:

*Naked I came from my mother's womb,*
*And naked shall I return there.*

*The LORD gave, and the LORD has taken away;*
*Blessed be the name of the LORD.*          Job 1:21

The Bible concludes:

*In all this Job did not sin, nor charge God with*
*wrong.*                          Job 1:22

I can't think of a more appropriate response. Can you? Job refused to blame God for his troubles. Since God is good, there had to be some other reason for it all. He might not understand it, but he knew that God was not to blame. That is a praiseworthy response.

## WHY DO YOU THINK?

Why do you think God allowed Satan to attack Job, when Job was His servant and an upright man? Let's continue the story to find the answer.

Satan again came into God's presence, and God said to him, as before:

*Have you considered My servant Job?*          Job 2:3

God was very pleased to inform Satan that His servant Job had maintained his integrity, even though Satan had attacked him without cause. This makes it even more clear that God allowed the attack on Job's family and his servants, even though He knew that Job was upright and had done nothing to deserve such an attack. God had a purpose in it. Now, there was to be another test.

## ANOTHER TEST

Satan remained obstinate and convinced, insisting to God that if he were allowed to attack Job's body, Job would curse Him to His face. Amazingly, God granted the wicked one that permission:

*And the LORD said to Satan, "Behold, he is in your hand, but spare his life."*                    Job 2:6

At that point, Satan caused boils to break out all over Job's body. One boil is bad enough, but Job had them *"from the sole of his foot to the crown of his head"* (Job 2:7). Before long, Job was suffering so terribly that his wife suggested to him that he curse God and go on and die. Job replied:

*Shall we indeed accept good from God, and shall we not accept adversity?*                    Job 2:10

Wow! What a response! This man was wise.
The chapter ends the same way the last one did:

*In all this Job did not sin with his lips.*         Job 2:10

Job still loved God, despite all that had happened to him, and he refused to blame Him for any of it. If God allowed it to happen, then there must be a good reason for it. That was Job's faith.

## A Whole Series of Tests

Was this the end of Job's trials? Hardly. The tales of his woes continue for forty more chapters, and by that time you would think Job would have taken his wife's advice and cursed God and died. But he didn't. He kept trusting God and moving forward, and finally, in Chapter 42, God intervened.

Job had passed all the tests, and now God began to restore to him all that had been lost. Before it was over, He gave him twice as much as he'd had before the attacks from Satan came. God blessed the end of Job's life more than his beginning. He gave him fourteen thousand sheep, six thousand camels, a thousand yoke of oxen, and a thousand donkeys. Job also had seven more sons and three more daughters. When he eventually died, he had lived one hundred and forty fruitful years.

## Now, What Do You Think?

So, now what do you think? Why did God allow Satan to attack Job? Personally, I believe that Job's perseverance in serving and loving God, no matter what came against him, brought glory to God and served as a wonderful testimony to all those around him, as it continues to do for us today.

God, our Creator, deserves all honor and glory. Job loved and honored God so much that he remained steadfast in his worship of Him, regardless of what happened to him. And that's what God wants for us too. Let us be so committed to Him that we will praise Him and love Him and serve Him all the days of our lives, no matter what we are required to go through. What could possibly happen to you that would be bad enough to cause you to turn against the God of the Universe? Nothing!

## NOTHING SHOULD DETER US

There should be nothing that would cause you or me to turn against God. So, can God depend on you?

It is apparent from Job's story that what Satan meant for evil, God turned around for good. And it can be the same with you. God loves you so much that He will sometimes allow hard things to come to your life. His purpose may simply be to cause you to turn to Him. He knows that if you go on "doing your own thing," you will never attain to the greater things He has planned for your life.

God has all the answers you need in life. He is the Alpha and the Omega, the beginning and the end! He has all the wisdom you need to live a blessed and fulfilled life. He is your Creator, He is your Father, and He wants the best for you.

Think about this: if everything were perfect in your life, would you need God? That's important. God wants us to need Him. He wants us to love Him. He wants us to trust Him, just as a child trusts his or her father. Earthly fathers fail and sometimes have wrong motives, but our heavenly Father never does. Let's learn to trust Him as Job did.

Now, let's look at another opposite of God and see if we can find the answers to our common question, *Why, God?*.

**Why, God?**

# CHAPTER 3

# WHY A FLOOD DESTROYED THE EARTH

*And he called his name Noah, saying, "This one will comfort us concerning our work and the toil of our hands, because of the ground which the LORD has cursed."*                                Genesis 5:29

Another Old Testament character who experienced the strange way God works was Noah. Son of Lamech, Noah's name meant "rest," and his father named him this because he believed that as a man his son would bring the people of God rest from their toils and distresses.

## BORN IN A DIFFICULT TIME

Noah was born into a very a difficult time. Wickedness had become so rampant upon the earth that God actually became sorry that He had created man in the first place. He was grieved because He so wanted men to seek after Him and His righteousness and not after the wicked one and sin. Because of the prevailing attitude of the day, God vowed to destroy the beautiful earth He had made and His crowning creation, man, with it:

> *So the Lord said, "I will destroy man whom I have created from the face of the earth, both man and beast, creeping thing and birds of the air, for I am sorry that I have made them."*                    Genesis 6:7

Thankfully, that very grave declaration was followed by a *but*, and the *but* concerned Noah and his reprieve:

> *But Noah found grace in the eyes of the Lord.*
>                                           Genesis 6:8

Grace can be defined as God's unmerited favor, but it also means God's acceptance and His goodwill. Noah was accepted by God and was blessed by His goodwill, and there was a reason for it.

## A JUST AND PERFECT MAN

Like Job, Noah was said to be a *"just"* and *"perfect"* man, one who *"walked with God"* (Genesis 6:9). This simply means that he chose a lifestyle of being in a close relationship with his Creator. And that was certainly pleasing to God. Was this not the reason He had created man in the first place?

Because Noah found grace in God's eyes, and God had determined to bring destruction upon the earth, He instructed this just man to build an ark, a boat of sorts, in order to save his life and the lives of his family members. God revealed to Noah that He would now flood the earth, and that this unprecedented flood would destroy all living flesh. Again, this drastic measure was being taken because of the extreme wickedness and violence of the age. But you know the story ... . Noah and his family built the ark, and they built it exactly as the Lord instructed them.

Upon the ark's completion, Noah and his wife and children (and their wives and children), along with the many animals God instructed them to bring with them, boarded the ark. Inside they would be safe, while outside all other men and beasts would perish in the flood.

## GOD MADE A COVENANT WITH NOAH

In doing this, God established a covenant with Noah. A covenant between God and man is an alliance of friendship, a binding agreement on both parties, signifying that they will each stand with the other until death. God was serious, and Noah was too.

After Noah, his family, and the animals were on the ark, and the door was shut, the waters of the deep began to rise, and the windows of Heaven were opened, and what followed was a great flood, the greatest of all floods. The Heavens poured out water for the next forty days, and all of those who were not safely in the ark perished.

It was only after the flood waters had remained on the earth for one hundred and fifty days that God caused a wind to come upon the earth, and the waters began to go down.

## Noah Was Grateful

Eventually, after what must have seemed like an eternity on board that small ark, Noah and his family and the animals they had preserved left the vessel, and the first thing Noah did was to build an altar to the Lord and make a sacrifice to Him.

God accepted Noah's offering and said that He would never again curse the ground or smite all of mankind at once because of sin. As proof of this, He promised to set a rainbow in the cloud. It would be a token of God's covenant agreement with man. Whenever He would see the rainbow He would remember the covenant, and never flood the earth again with the intention of destroying all flesh.

## Why?

What a very strange series of events. Why do you think God went to so much trouble to destroy wicked men and to save the few righteous? He could have just burned up those who were in sin and rebellion against Him and, at the same time, spared Noah and his family. Here we see, as always, that God's ways are much higher than our ways, and His thoughts are much higher than our thoughts. He has declared it to be so:

*For as the heavens are higher than the earth,*
*So are My ways higher than your ways,*
*And My thoughts than your thoughts.*     Isaiah 55:9

Personally, I believe that Noah's ark was a sign of a future deliverance for mankind, a way of escape for you and me.

An ark was also used as a means of deliverance from destruction for Moses, when he was still just a small infant. Let's take a look at that story, another opposite of God, to see if we can find the answers to our common question, *Why, God?*.

# CHAPTER 4

# WHY A CHILD WAS CHOSEN TO BE THE DELIVERER

*But God has chosen the foolish things of the world to put to shame the wise, and God has chosen the weak things of the world to put to shame the things which are mighty.*                    1 Corinthians 1:27

God used Moses in ways that defy our human thinking, but always remember that God is love, and everything He does is motivated by that love.

Moses was used to deliver the people of Israel after four hundred years of slavery at the hands of the Egyptians. God used unusual methods to do this, and He used this unlikely man, and He did it to show His love to His people.

To this very day, God continues to use unusual methods and unlikely people to show us His love, and He wants to use you too.

## Why Does God Want to Confound the Wise and Mighty?

But why would God want to *"confound"* (KJV) or *"put to shame"* the *"wise"* and the *"mighty"*? It's because God loves the sinner and knows that if he or she persists in their own wisdom and might, they will experience continual hardship and destruction in their lives. Remember, God is love.

The wisdom of the world says "Only the strong survive" and "It's the survival of the fittest." Paul, the apostle, however, contradicted that. He said:

*When I am weak, then I am strong.*

2 Corinthians 12:10

What did he mean by that? He meant that humility always brings us God's favor. If we are wise in our own eyes, we are doomed to failure.

### The Beginnings of Moses' Story

The story of Moses is recorded in the Old Testament, beginning in the first chapter of Exodus. There we see that after the children of Israel had been in bondage in Egypt for hundreds of years, a new king, or Pharaoh, came to power. This Pharaoh was concerned because the Israelites were growing so fast in numbers. He feared that if there arose a war against one of his enemies, the Israelites might join that enemy against him. Using this as a pretext, he began to afflict them with great burdens. Still they multiplied.

Next, to control the growth of the Jews, Pharaoh ordered the Hebrew midwives to kill all the newborn sons, and just let the daughters live. We know that Satan was influencing the thoughts of Pharaoh in this because God hates murder.

The Hebrew midwives disobeyed Pharaoh, and he asked them why they had failed to kill the sons, as he had ordered. They told him that the Hebrew women delivered so quickly that they were unable to get there in time. By the time they arrived, it was already too late. The son would be born. The Bible shows us that this pleased God:

*God dealt well with the midwives: and the people multiplied, and grew very mighty.* Exodus 1:20

So, despite Pharaoh's attempts, the people of God continued to prosper. Pharaoh, however, did not give up. Now he instructed his people to throw every newborn Hebrew son into the river (and this is where Moses comes into the picture).

Moses' father, a Levite, was married to a daughter of Levi. Together they bore a son, and they hid him for three months so that he would not be killed by the Egyptians, sensing that God had a great destiny for this boy. And He did. He gave Moses' parents a plan that saved the child's life.

## A Plan that Saved His Life

When Moses' mother was no longer able to hide him, she made an ark of bulrushes, covered it with pitch to waterproof it, and then placed it at the edge of the river so that Pharaoh's daughter would find it. Soon Pharaoh's daughter came to bathe in the river, and she saw the ark floating there in the water, and sent her maids to get it.

When the ark was opened, and Pharaoh's daughter saw the child, he was crying, and her womanly heart was touched. She had compassion on Moses in that moment, even though she could clearly see that he was a Hebrew child:

*This is one of the Hebrew's children.*      Exodus 2:6

Moses' sister, who just happened to be one of the woman's maids, asked her if she should go find a nurse from among the Hebrew women to nurse the child.

Do you suppose that it was a coincidence that the child's very sister was serving as a maid for Pharaoh's daughter? And which Hebrew woman do you think she found to nurse the child? Yes, she brought back Moses' own mother. God is always in complete control of every situation, and He knew what He was doing in this case.

## Raised by His Own Mother

When Moses' mother was brought, Pharaoh's daughter told her to take the child and nurse him and even paid her to do it. How about that?

When the child was older, the mother then took him back to Pharaoh's daughter, and he became her legal son. She called him Moses because he was drawn out of the water (the name *Moses* means "drawn"). This saving of the life of Moses, by the use of the ark and God's unusual plan, was the first step in the deliverance of the children of Israel from slavery in Egypt and their possession of the land that God had promised to Abraham and his descendants. What an awesome God we serve!

## BUT, WHY?

But why do you think God went to all the trouble of setting up Moses as the deliverer of His people? Couldn't He have chosen some adult from among the people of Israel? The answer is no. Would Pharaoh have ever allowed a Hebrew slave to approach his throne to make intercession for the people of Israel? No way. But, because of the infinite wisdom of God, Israel was freed from the bondage of the Egyptians.

Because Pharaoh's daughter took a Hebrew boy to be her son, Moses grew up in the courts of the king and was taught in the ways of the Egyptians. The New Testament book of Acts describes the life of Moses in the house of Pharaoh:

*And Moses was learned in all the wisdom of the Egyptians, and was mighty in words and in deeds.*

Acts 7:22

**35**

## The Activation of His Calling

When Moses was forty years old, he visited his brothers—the children of Israel. He saw that one of his brothers was treated wrongly by an Egyptian, so he killed the Egyptian. When Pharaoh heard about this, he sought to kill Moses, but Moses fled Egypt and went to the land of Midian. The book of Hebrews records:

*By faith Moses, when he became of age, refused to be called the son of Pharaoh's daughter, choosing rather to suffer affliction with the people of God than to enjoy the passing pleasures of sin, esteeming the reproach of Christ greater riches than the treasures in Egypt; for he looked to the reward. By faith he forsook Egypt, not fearing the wrath of the king; for he endured as seeing Him who is invisible.* Hebrews 11:24-27

God's way is always to use people of faith, those who believe without seeing, to accomplish His purposes. Will you be a person of faith?

Always remember that Jesus is *"the author and finisher of our faith"* (Hebrews 12:2) and that *"faith comes by hearing, and hearing by the Word of God"* (Romans 10:17). When will we learn to trust in God's wisdom and not our own?

God made you. He is your Creator. He knows everything about you. He loves you and wants the best for you. He has a perfect plan, designed specifically for your life and your personality. He has given you gifts and talents to be used for His glory. Let me encourage you to open up your heart to Him right now. Say "yes" to Him and to His plan for your life.

## MOSES FLED

Now, let's look further at some of the unusual ways that God used Moses. After Moses fled to the land of Midian, he married a daughter of Jethro, the priest of Midian and had a son. Moses was keeping the flock of his father-in-law and led the flock to the backside of the desert, to the mountain of God called Horeb. An angel of the Lord appeared to Moses out of the middle of a bush that was burning but not consumed.

When Moses turned aside, out of curiosity, to see why the bush was not consumed, God called out his name twice. The Lord told him to take off his shoes, because the ground he was standing on was holy ground. God spoke to Moses and told him that He had seen the affliction of His people in Egypt and was aware of their sorrows. He told Moses that He would now send him to Pharaoh to deliver the Israelites out of Egypt into the land that had been promised to Abraham, a land flowing with milk and honey.

## MOSES' EXCUSES

All of this was hard for Moses to accept. He answered God:

*Who am I that I should go to Pharaoh, and that I should bring the children of Israel out of Egypt?*

Exodus 3:11

God answered back that He would be with Moses and that it would be a token for him. Well, if God is for you, who can be against you! Isn't it wonderful that if you are a Christian, the Bible promises that Christ is *"in you"*:

*To them God willed to make known what are the riches of the glory of this mystery among the Gentiles: which is Christ in you, the hope of glory.* Colossians 1:27

It also promises:

*Ye are of God, little children, and have overcome them: because greater is he that is in you, than he that is in the world.* 1 John 4:4

With God, all things are possible, and nothing is impossible to those who believe in Jesus Christ! It was time for Moses to drop his excuses, and it's time for us to do the same.

## WHO HAS SENT ME?

Moses next asked the Lord who he should say had sent him:

*Then Moses said to God, "Indeed, when I come to the*

*children of Israel and say to them, 'The God of your fathers has sent me to you,' and they say to me, 'What is His name?' what shall I say to them?"*

Exodus 3:13

The answer God gave Moses that day was clear and powerful:

*And God said to Moses, "I AM WHO I AM." And He said, "Thus you shall say to the children of Israel, 'I AM has sent me to you.'"*

Exodus 3:14

Our God is the great *"I AM."* He always was and always will be, and His Kingdom is without end. Isn't it interesting that Jesus used these identical words when He declared who *He* was:

*Jesus said to him, "I am the way, the truth, and the life. No one comes to the Father except through Me.*

John 14:6

Jesus is the Great I AM.

God told Moses further that day that he was to tell the people:

*The LORD God of your fathers, the God of Abraham, the God of Isaac, and the God of Jacob, has sent me to you. This is My name forever, and this is My memorial to all generations.*

Exodus 3:15

**39**

## Providing Signs and Wonders

When Moses continued to make excuses, saying that the people would not believe that God had appeared to him, God showed him some signs and wonders he could use to convince the king (and any other doubter).

First God told Moses to throw down his rod, and when he did, it became a snake. Next, God told him to place his hand in the waist of his garment, and when he drew it out it had become leprous like snow. God said to put his hand back into his garment and pull it out again, and when he did that, it became normal again.

If the people would not believe these signs, God told Moses, then he was to take some of the water of the Nile River and pour it on the dry land, and the water would turn into blood. He would not run out of miraculous signs.

## One Final Excuse Is Silenced

Moses came up with one more excuse as to why he should not be the one to deliver Israel. He told God that he was *"slow of speech"* and *"slow of tongue," "not eloquent"* (Exodus 4:10). God countered these excuses by saying to Moses:

*Who has made man's mouth? Or who makes the mute, the deaf, the seeing, or the blind? Have not I, the Lord?* Exodus 4:11

**40**

Next God said:

*I will be with your mouth and teach you what you shall say.* Exodus 4:12

Still, after all of this, Moses continued to stall, so God said that if he insisted, he could put words in the mouth of his brother Aaron, and Aaron would become his spokesperson. This left Moses with no more excuses, so God sent him on his way back to Egypt.

## Pharaoh Refused

When Moses arrived in Egypt, he and Aaron wasted no time in approaching Pharaoh with the demand that he let God's people go. Pharaoh refused, and he continued to refuse again and again. As a result, God brought ten terrible plagues upon the people of Egypt (these plagues can be studied in the book of Exodus).

Each of the plagues that came upon the Egyptians was aimed directly at one of their false gods. For example, the first plague turned the water of the Nile River into blood. Because this river was a source of life for the Egyptians, they considered it to be sacred. God turned it into something dead.

With another plague, frogs overran the land. These frogs came from the same river, so they were considered gods also.

Pharaoh's son was also considered a god by the Egyptians, and his life was taken from him in the final plague.

Through the use of each of the ten plagues, God was showing the people of Egypt that their so-called gods were no gods at all. He was the only true God.

Since the Israelites had been in bondage in Egypt for four hundred years, they, too, may have worshipped some of these false gods at one time or another. So at the same time God was speaking to the Egyptians, He was showing His people, too, that He was the *only* true and living God.

## FREED AT LAST

Finally, after ten plagues, Pharaoh let the people of Israel go into the wilderness, and their journey to the Promised Land began. Still, even though he had let them go, Pharaoh followed them into the wilderness. There God parted the Red Sea to allow His people to cross over safely and escape, and when the Egyptians dared to follow them, the waters closed and covered them, and they were destroyed.

God did one miracle after another in the desert for His people. He gave them manna from Heaven and quails that flew into the camp for them to eat. He made water flow out of a rock for them to drink. He performed many other miracles to take care of them, and He did it all because of His love for them. Our God is a God of miracles, and His ways are high above our ways. His way is love. The Psalmist David declared:

*God made known His ways unto Moses, His acts unto the children of Israel.*          Psalm 103:7

Would you rather know the *"acts"* of God or to know His *"ways"*? Jesus said:

*An evil and adulterous generation seeks after a sign, and no sign will be given to it except the sign of the prophet Jonah.*          Matthew 12:39

These words are also recorded in Matthew 16:4. What does this mean?

A *sign* is the equivalent of an *act*. An evil generation seeks after signs or acts from God, when what God wants is for us to seek to know His *ways*.

What, then, was *"the sign of the prophet Jonah"*? Let's look now at Jonah's story to see if we can better understand God's ways and find the answers to our common question, *Why, God?*.

Why, God?

# CHAPTER 5

# WHY A "BIG FISH" SWALLOWED A PROPHET

*Now the LORD had prepared a great fish to swallow Jonah. And Jonah was in the belly of the fish three days and three nights.*                    Jonah 1:17

In the case of Jonah, God shows us another way that He directs his child in order to accomplish His purposes, and, at the same time, develop his character. God is always concerned with helping us to develop a more godly character. And He always wants to show His love for the world by using us.

## WHO WAS JONAH?

Jonah was a prophet of God and the son of the prophet Amittai. God spoke to Jonah and told him to go to the great city of Nineveh, capital of the ancient Kingdom of Assyria. Nineveh was located about two hundred and fifty miles north of Babylon, on the east bank of the

Tigris River. God saw the wickedness of Nineveh and, because of His love for the people there, He wanted Jonah to prophesy against the city, so that its inhabitants would repent of their ways and turn to Him.

**God knows that if we choose the easy way of sin, destruction will come to our lives.** Satan, our enemy, knows this also, and he entices us to have our own way. Jesus said:

*The thief does not come except to steal, and to kill, and to destroy. I have come that they may have life, and that they may have it more abundantly.* John 10:10

Jonah took the easy way out and fled from the presence of the Lord to Tarshish. The ancient city of Tarshish was probably near Spain on the Mediterranean Sea. Jonah went to Joppa first, and there he boarded a ship that would take him on to Tarshish.

The reason Jonah fled from God was that he didn't want to go to Nineveh. He understood that God wanted the Ninevites to repent and turn to Him, but Jonah wanted Him to destroy the Ninevites because of their wickedness.

## GOD SENT A GREAT WIND AGAINST THE SHIP

After the ship on which Jonah had embarked set sail for Tarshish, God brought a mighty wind against it, and the seas began raging, so much that the ship was about to break up. The mariners were afraid and started throwing the cargos they were hauling overboard, to lighten the ship. Meanwhile, Jonah was fast asleep below deck.

The captain went below and woke Jonah up and told him to call upon his God, so that they would not die. Then the mariners cast lots to see who was responsible for the storm coming upon them in the first place. The lot fell upon Jonah.

Now the men set about to ask Jonah what the cause of this evil that had come upon them could be. They asked him where he was from and what his occupation was. He told them that he was a Hebrew and that he feared the Lord, the God of Heaven, who made the sea and the dry land. When they knew that he was running from God, they became very frightened and asked him why he had brought this evil upon them all.

Next they asked Jonah what they should do to him to make the sea become calm again. He told them to throw him into the sea. That, he said, would bring the calm. The men didn't want to do that, so they continued rowing, but when the tempest did not stop, they eventually felt compelled to do it. When they had thrown Jonah overboard, the sea was calmed, just as he had said it would be.

## God Had Prepared "a Great Fish"

God had already prepared what the Bible calls *"a great fish"* to swallow Jonah, and he was in the belly of that great fish for the next three days and three nights. We can only imagine what that must have been like. At the very least, we can say that it was a terrible experience.

**47**

Then, when he had suffered in this way for three days and nights, from the bottom of the fish's belly, Jonah called out to God and said that he would look again toward His holy temple. He said that he would sacrifice unto God with the voice of thanksgiving and pay what he had vowed. At the end of his prayers he said:

*Salvation is of the Lord.*                          Jonah 2:9

At that point, God spoke to the fish, and he vomited Jonah out onto the dry land. Wow! What a story!

## WHAT WE LEARN FROM THIS

What we learn from this is that God had a specific purpose for Jonah and had to prepare him for his task. He now spoke to Jonah the second time and told him to arise and go to Nineveh to preach against their wickedness and to tell them to repent. This time, Jonah went.

It took Jonah three days to reach the city, and as he entered it, he began to cry out the message of God:

*Yet forty days, and Nineveh shall be overthrown.*
                                        Jonah 3:4

What do you think the response of the people was? The Bible says that they believed God and proclaimed a fast, and put on sackcloth, and sat in ashes. This was their way of repenting. Not only did the people repent, but even the King took off his royal robes and covered himself with sackcloth and ashes. He also made a decree that no one, including the animals, would eat or drink water during the time of seeking God. He said further that everyone in the kingdom was to repent and turn from violence and then expressed the hope that God would change His mind and not destroy the city.

When God saw the repentant spirit of the people of Nineveh, He did change His mind and did not destroy the city, as Jonah had predicted would happen. This brings to mind the promise of God in 2 Chronicles 7:14:

*If my people, which are called by my name, shall humble themselves, and pray, and seek my face, and turn from their wicked ways; then will I hear from heaven, and will forgive their sin, and will heal their land.* (KJV)

Even that wicked nation of Nineveh repented and turned from its wicked ways, and when it did, God healed the land. Today, many in America, as well as in other nations, are living lives separated from God. Wickedness prevails. Sin abounds. There is social injustice, hatred, jealousy, and all other forms of evil. However, even while all of these things are present, there is a remnant of people who love God and love others so much that they are willing to pray and repent so that God will heal our lands.

Remember, God loves you and desires to know you personally. He has a plan for your life, which He wants to share with you. God's way for your life is the *best* way!

## Jonah's Disappointment

Well, you might think that Jonah was overjoyed by the response of the people of Nineveh. But quite the contrary, he was angry. He now complained to God that he had fled his own country to avoid going to Nineveh in the first place, precisely because he knew that God was a merciful and kind God, who was slow to anger. He knew that God would change His mind about destroying the city, if the people repented, and he had wanted them to be destroyed instead.

Even today, many would like for sinners to be destroyed or punished, not remembering that they themselves are also sinners. Christians should not be in this group. We should hate the sin and Satan, the author of sin, but love the sinner.

You would think that after experiencing the mercy of God for himself, when he was rescued from the belly of the fish, Jonah would also have had mercy on the Ninevites. Actually he asked God to take his life rather than see the people of Nineveh restored.

But God didn't take Jonah's life. What He did do was to show Jonah that he should be more like Him, showing mercy, and not vengeance. God did this by preparing a gourd, as a covering, to protect Jonah from the heat. He had left the city proper and was waiting outside of it to see what would happen. He was thankful for the gourd, but then God prepared a worm to eat the gourd.

As we so often say, "God works in mysterious ways." The next day God prepared a strong east wind, and the sun beat down on Jonah so that he wanted to die. God then asked him if he was angry because the gourd had withered, and he replied:

*It is better for me to die than to live.*     Jonah 4:8

God answered Jonah and pointed out the fact that he'd had pity on the gourd, which he had not made himself, but he refused to have pity on the people of the great city of Nineveh, people created in the image of God.

On the other hand, God had pity for the people of the city, even though they were steeped in sin and wickedness. This shows us an important truth: **God hates sin but loves sinners**. In all of this, God was teaching Jonah that he was to have an attitude of love and forgiveness for others, no matter how they acted. Unforgiveness causes pain and anguish in our lives (we'll discuss the power of forgiveness in a later chapter).

## IT'S ALL TRUE

It is important to realize that all that is related in this story of Jonah really happened. This is not just a fable. And the lessons to be learned from the story have to do with love, forgiveness, mercy, and compassion. Jesus even mentioned the story during His ministry on earth:

*And while the crowds were thickly gathered together, He began to say, "This is an evil generation. It seeks a sign, and no sign will be given to it except the sign of Jonah the prophet. For as Jonah became a sign to the Ninevites, so also the Son of Man will be to this generation. The queen of the South will rise up in the judgment with the men of this generation and condemn them, for she came from the ends of the earth to hear the wisdom of Solomon; and indeed a greater than Solomon is here. The men of Nineveh will rise up in the judgment with this generation and condemn it, for they repented at the preaching of Jonah; and indeed a greater than Jonah is here."*　　　Luke 11:29-32

In this passage, Jesus was speaking of Himself. He is the Greater One that was to come!

The Ninevites, He said, were an evil generation, and yet they received *"the sign of the prophet Jonah."* Just as Jonah was in the belly of the fish for three days and three nights and then came to the city, preaching that the people should repent of their sins so that they could be saved from destruction, Jesus Christ died and was buried in the belly of the earth for three days and three nights and then came forth to preach repentance from sin so that the people of His day could be saved from destruction as well. This was *"the sign of the prophet Jonah."*

## THE MESSAGE OF REPENTANCE IS FOR TODAY

This message of repentance still applies today, and it's for me and for you. When John the Baptist appeared, this was also his message:

*Repent for the kingdom of heaven is at hand.*
Matthew 3:2

Jesus told the people of His day about some Galileans whose blood Pilate had mingled with their sacrifices, and He said of their death:

*Unless you repent, you will all likewise perish.*
Luke 13:3

Jesus also told of eighteen people on whom the Tower of Siloam had fallen. They died, He said, and then He repeated:

*Unless you repent you will all likewise perish.*
Luke 13:5

In both of these cases, Jesus said, the people involved were no greater sinners that others. So unless we repent, we will also perish.

All of us are sinners, and all of us will die physically someday, but it is not necessary to die spiritually, meaning that we would be doomed to a life of everlasting torment in Hell. Jesus made a way of escape for us. We'll talk about this way of escape in the last chapter of the book.

Next, let's look at a marvelous example of forgiveness in the Bible—the story of Joseph—to learn more about God's ways and see if we can find the answers to our common question, *Why, God?.*

# CHAPTER 6

# WHY JOSEPH
# WAS MISTREATED

*Now Israel loved Joseph more than all his children, because he was the son of his old age. Also he made him a tunic of many colors.* Genesis 37:3

Joseph was the youngest son of Israel, whose name had been changed from Jacob, and his story is one of forgiveness. It takes up many chapters of Genesis, the book of beginnings.

Israel loved his son Joseph because he was the son of his old age, so he made him a coat of many colors. When Joseph's brothers saw how much their father loved Joseph, they were jealous and hated Joseph, and could not speak peaceably to him.

## JOSEPH WAS A DREAMER

Joseph had a dream, which he proceeded to tell to his brothers. He said that, in the dream, they were binding sheaves (bundles of grain) in a field, and he saw his sheaf rise and stand up and then his brothers' sheaves stood up and bowed down to his sheaf. The brothers asked Joseph if he intended to reign over them, and from that time on, they hated him even more. They hated him for his dream, and they hated him for his words.

To add insult to injury, Joseph had another dream, and he also told this one to his brothers. He said that, in the dream, the sun, moon, and stars bowed down to him. He told this dream to his father, and his father rebuked him and asked him if the whole family should come and bow down to him. Still, Israel wasn't sure what to think of Joseph's dreaming. The end result was that Joseph's brothers envied him all the more, but his father kept an open mind to all this dreaming.

## LOOK, THIS DREAMER IS COMING

The brothers went off to feed their father's sheep in Shechem, and after a time, Israel sent Joseph to check on them and the flocks they tended. When his brothers saw him coming from a distance, they mocked him, saying, *"Look, this dreamer is coming"* (Genesis 37:19). They quickly put together a plan to kill their brother. Then they would tell their father that a wild animal had done it.

Fortunately, Reuben one of the eldest of the brothers, intervened. He suggested that they not actually kill Joseph. Just throw him into a pit, and let things take their course. So, it was decided. They stripped from Joseph the coat of many colors his father had given him, and they threw him into an empty pit.

## SOLD INTO SLAVERY

This done, the brothers sat down to eat. When they next looked up, they saw a caravan of merchants coming, and, knowing that the merchants were on their way to Egypt to sell their wares, they got an idea. They could sell Joseph to the merchants, ridding themselves of him once and for all, and making a little cash in the process.

And the idea worked. The merchants bought Joseph from his brothers for twenty pieces of silver, and they brought him down to Egypt to be sold into slavery there.

Reuben was unaware of what the others had done, and when he later returned to the pit and found Joseph missing, he was in anguish and tore his clothes. The brothers decided to kill a goat and put the goat's blood on Joseph's coat and then bring it back to their father.

Again, their plan worked. When Israel saw the coat, he took it for granted that a wild animal had killed Joseph, and he, too, tore his clothes, put on sackcloth, and mourned for many days. He had so loved this son that he refused to be comforted.

## SOLD TO POTIPHAR

Meanwhile, the merchants turned their money over by selling Joseph to a man named Potiphar, one of Pharaoh's officers, and captain of the guard. But during the time he spent as a slave in Egypt, God blessed Joseph and prospered all that he touched, and Potiphar, his master, couldn't help but notice it. Thus, Joseph found grace in his master's eyes, and Potiphar put him in control of his household and his possessions. That was a wise move, for now God blessed Potiphar because of Joseph, and Joseph became even more favored.

## TROUBLE WAS BREWING

Then one day Potiphar's wife approached Joseph and asked him to have sexual relations with her. He refused, saying, *"How can I do this great wickedness, and sin against God"?* (Genesis 39:9). But she wouldn't leave it alone. She kept asking him to lie with her day by day. He continued to refuse. Then one day, she grabbed him by his garment, in an attempt to force her will upon him, but he ran away, leaving the garment behind.

The woman told all the men of the house (and later her husband) that Joseph had approached her, to have sexual relations, and that she had screamed, and he ran off leaving his outer garment. When he heard this, Potiphar was understandably angry with Joseph and put him into a prison, where the king's prisoners were kept.

What a terrible injustice this was! But God was with Joseph and showed him favor in the sight of the prison keeper. As a result, the man put Joseph in charge of all the other prisoners.

## Prospering Even in Prison

Sometime later, it happened that Pharaoh's butler and baker offended him, and he put them in the same prison where Joseph was being kept. The captain of the guard put Joseph in charge of them, and, rather than use his authority over them, he served them.

One night the butler and the baker both had a dream. The next morning, when Joseph came to serve them, he noticed that they were sad. He asked them why, and they said that they'd each had a dream that they didn't understand. Joseph said to them: *"Do not interpretations belong to God?"* (Genesis 40:8). He then asked them to tell him the dreams, and he was able to interpret them.

According to the butler's dream, his life would be spared, and his position would be restored to him within three days. According to the baker's dream, Pharaoh would have him hanged in three days. All of what Joseph said came to pass.

## Remember Me

Before the butler was released, Joseph asked him to please mention his situation to Pharaoh, but two more years went by before the man remembered to do it. Pharaoh had two dreams and was troubled by them, so he called for the magicians and wise men of Egypt to interpret them for him. They were unable to do so, and then the butler remembered Joseph and spoke of him to the king. He reminded Pharaoh how he had been put into prison, along with the baker, and he told Pharaoh of the dreams he and the baker had had and how Joseph had correctly interpreted them. Immediately, Pharaoh called for Joseph and asked him to interpret his dreams.

## JOSEPH IS TAKEN BEFORE PHARAOH

Joseph first told Pharaoh it was not he who had the interpretation, but that God would give him an answer. Then the king told him the two dreams, and Joseph told the Pharaoh the interpretation: Egypt would have seven years of plenty, followed by seven years of famine.

The reason there were two dreams, Joseph said, was so that the thing would be established and shortly come to pass. Joseph advised Pharaoh to store up food during the seven good years so that there would be food during the famine.

Pharaoh was very pleased with all that Joseph said, and he made him ruler over Egypt, only second to himself. This was remarkable, for many reasons. For one thing, Joseph was only thirty years old, and another was that he was a Hebrew. Isn't that just like God to take a young man from obscurity, one who was sold into slavery, and place him in the second highest position in Egypt? Jesus said to His disciples:

*If anyone desires to be first, he shall be last of all and servant of all.*                                    Mark 9:35

*You know that those who are considered rulers over the*

*Gentiles lord it over them, and their great ones exercise authority over them. Yet it shall not be so among you; but whoever desires to become great among you shall be your servant. And whoever of you desires to be first shall be slave of all. For even the Son of Man did not come to be served, but to serve, and to give His life a ransom for many.*                                    Mark 10:42-45

These two passages speak for themselves. In Luke 19, Jesus told an interesting parable. It is a lengthy passage, but it is worth reading:

*Now as they heard these things, He spoke another parable, because He was near Jerusalem and because they thought the kingdom of God would appear immediately. Therefore He said: "A certain nobleman went into a far country to receive for himself a kingdom and to return. So he called ten of his servants, delivered to them ten minas, and said to them, 'Do business till I come.' But his citizens hated him, and sent a delegation after him, saying, 'We will not have this man to reign over us.'*
*"And so it was that when he returned, having received the kingdom, he then commanded these servants, to whom he had given the money, to be called to him, that he might know how much every man had gained by trading. Then came the first, saying, 'Master, your mina has earned ten minas.' And he said to him, 'Well done, good servant; because you were faithful in a very little, have authority over ten cities.' And the second came, saying, 'Master, your mina has earned*

*five minas.' Likewise he said to him, 'You also be over five cities.'*

*"Then another came, saying, 'Master, here is your mina, which I have kept put away in a handkerchief. For I feared you, because you are an austere man. You collect what you did not deposit, and reap what you did not sow.' And he said to him, 'Out of your own mouth I will judge you, you wicked servant. You knew that I was an austere man, collecting what I did not deposit and reaping what I did not sow. Why then did you not put my money in the bank, that at my coming I might have collected it with interest?'*

*"And he said to those who stood by, 'Take the mina from him, and give it to him who has ten minas.' (But they said to him, 'Master, he has ten minas.') 'For I say to you, that to everyone who has will be given; and from him who does not have, even what he has will be taken away from him. But bring here those enemies of mine, who did not want me to reign over them, and slay them before me.' "*                          Luke 19:11-27

So, just like Joseph, those who are faithful in small acts of service will be given authority over great things in the Kingdom of God.

## YOUR HOPE

Remember, God does things "opposite" from the way we do things. Wouldn't you rather do things His way? He has the very *best* plan for your life. He said in His Word:

*For I know the thoughts that I think toward you, says the LORD, thoughts of peace and not of evil, to give you a future and a hope.* Jeremiah 29:11

This word *expected,* in original Hebrew, means "things hoped for." In other words, **God thinks about you. And what He thinks about you is giving you peace and fulfilling your hopes and dreams.** Knowing these facts should give you great joy and peace in your heart!

Because we humans often live our day-to-day lives without asking God how He wants us to live, we may miss out on His best for us. Yes, He is in control, but He does not interfere with our free will. Knowing that God does many things opposite from the way we do should cause us to ask Him each day how He wants us to function, so that we may fulfill our purpose.

Joseph was a young man living in obscurity, but God lifted him up to become a man of great influence and leadership. He became a blessing to the Egyptians, as well as the Israelites. (The rest of Joseph's story, of how restoration came to him and his family can be found in Genesis chapters 41-45.)

Another young man whom God lifted up to be King over Israel was David. He was a shepherd and only a boy when God called him. Let's now take a look at his life, to see if we can learn more about God's ways and find the answers to our common question, *Why, God?.*

# CHAPTER 7

# WHY GOD MADE A SHEPHERD BOY KING

*How long will you mourn for Saul, seeing I have rejected him from reigning over Israel? Fill your horn with oil, and go; I am sending you to Jesse the Bethlehemite. For I have provided Myself a king among his sons.*

1 Samuel 16:1

David was the son of Jesse, and Jesse was the son of Obed. This is significant because Obed was the son of Boaz and his famous wife Ruth.

Ruth was a Moabitess and not a Hebrew at all. In the next chapter, we will discuss how God used Ruth in an unusual way to further His plans for Israel. She became part of the lineage of David and, ultimately, of Jesus, the Messiah! For now, let's look at how and why God picked David, a humble shepherd boy, to become king over Israel.

## SAMUEL'S PART IN THE DRAMA

The story begins with the prophet Samuel. He was mourning because of how Israel's first king, King Saul, had turned out, when God approached him and told him to go to the house of Jesse and there pick the next king of Israel from among Jesse's sons. Samuel went as instructed.

When Jesse brought his firstborn son before Samuel, thinking that he would surely become the next king, God spoke to the prophet and said,

> *Do not look at his appearance or at his physical stature, because I have refused him. For the LORD does not see as man sees; for man looks at the outward appearance, but the LORD looks at the heart.*
>
> 1 Samuel 16:7

Saul, who, again, was their first king, was taller than other men and looked the part of a king. God had not picked him, but had allowed the people to do it, and man's way is to pick leaders according to their looks, their ability at public speaking, or their intelligence. As God said, *"Man looks at the outward appearance."* God, however, does just the opposite. He looks at a person's heart.

Remember again that God's ways are above our ways and His thoughts are above our thoughts. God knows what He is doing, doesn't He?

## SIX MORE SONS REJECTED

Jesse brought six more of his sons before Samuel, and the result was that God did not choose any of them. Samuel then asked Jesse if he had no more children, and Jesse said that there was the youngest, David. He was off tending the sheep. Samuel told him to send for the boy, and when he had arrived, the Lord told Samuel to anoint him, because he was to be the next king.

This act of anointing with oil was for separation for service to God. So the prophet anointed David with oil, and the Scriptures declare:

> *And the Spirit of the LORD came upon David from that day forward.* 1 Samuel 16:13

But even though Samuel anointed David to be king of Israel, Saul was still ruling. He had disobeyed God and sinned, and Samuel had prophesied to him that the kingdom would be taken from him because of it.

## DAVID BECOMES SAUL'S ARMOR-BEARER

After Samuel had anointed David, the Spirit of God came upon him, and the Spirit of God left Saul, and, in its place, an evil, or distressing, spirit came upon him. Saul's servants saw his torment and suggested that he send for the son of Jesse, the one who tended the sheep, because, they said:

*Look, I have seen a son of Jesse the Bethlehemite, who
is skillful in playing, a mighty man of valor, a man of
war, prudent in speech, and a handsome person; and
the LORD is with him.*                    1 Samuel 16:18

I believe that God gave Saul's servants this idea. Out
of all of the people they could have been chosen, Saul
picked David. God is so awesome and so wise, and often
He orchestrates situations to accomplish His purposes. If
God didn't make Saul's servants think of David, they did
it anyway.

When this evil spirit that came upon Saul was mentioned in the Scriptures, it was called *"a distressing [evil,
KJV] spirit from the Lord"* Some may wonder how an evil
spirit, distressing or otherwise, could come *"from the
Lord,"* and why it would come upon Saul. God is all good
and all loving, but His purpose in permitting this thing
was to cause Saul to be in a position of needing comfort,
of needing David. So it was that David was sent for, and
he became Saul's armor-bearer. Whenever David saw that
King Saul was disturbed, he took his harp and played, and
Saul was refreshed, and the evil spirit left him.

## FACING THE MIGHTY GOLIATH

Soon enough, the Philistines came against Saul and Israel, and they sent their most powerful warrior, Goliath,
to taunt the Israelites. David was at home tending the
sheep, while his brothers were at the standoff between Israel and the Philistines. David may have wanted to go to

the battlefront with his brothers, but he was being faithful and obedient to his father by tending the sheep.

Here is a lesson for Christians: be faithful with what your spiritual leader has you doing, and, in God's time, you will be given greater things to do. Jesus taught His disciples:

*Well done, good and faithful servant; you were faithful over a few things, I will make you ruler over many things. Enter into the joy of your lord.*

Matthew 25:21

*He who is faithful in what is least is faithful also in much; and he who is unjust in what is least is unjust also in much.*                    Luke 16:10

## DAVID'S DAY CAME

One day David's father sent him to bring some food to his brothers and to see how the battle was going. The story is well known how David ended up killing the Philistine giant with a sling and a stone. Only God alone could make this happen.

Let me ask this question: when you are faced with "giants" that are opposing you in your life, what do you do? Your particular giants may be financial, emotional, spiritual, or any other looming problem that may cause you to have fear or confusion. David was a small, unarmed boy, and yet he took on the Philistine champion.

Goliath was prepared for any battle with weapons and

armor, but God had a plan. And God always has a plan for your life, as well. The Spirit of God instructed David to sling the stone at Goliath. At this, no doubt, he was an expert because he used the sling against wild animals that would threaten his sheep.

## Prepared for the Future

God had already prepared David for this momentous event that would deliver His people from the Philistine aggressors. And I believe that the things that have happened in your life (both good and bad) have prepared you for your future. If you are a Christian, God's promise to you is this:

> *And we know that all things work together for good to those who love God, to those who are the called according to His purpose.*　　　　　　Romans 8:28

This word *called* means "invited." You have been invited by God to be part of His Kingdom and His plan. Do you realize that the Almighty God of the Universe has a plan for your life? We saw in the last chapter how He said:

> *For I know the thoughts that I think toward you, saith the Lord, thoughts of peace and not of evil, to give you an expected end.*　　　　　　Jeremiah 29:11, KJV

Again, this word *expected* means "things hoped for." Do you need hope in your life? Do you need joy? Do you need a sense of purpose and fulfillment? God alone knows His thoughts about you and how His thoughts will lead you to these things. So, what do you do when you are faced with those "giants"? I believe that the only way to have victory is to call upon God for His help. Let me encourage you to reach out to Him right now and ask Him to help you. Ask Him to come into your life and be your Lord.

Accept Jesus Christ as your Savior:

*Believe on the Lord Jesus Christ, and you will be saved.*                              Acts 16:31

Later in this book, we will look at why we need a Savior and why Jesus is that Savior. He is the Messiah.

## David's Reign

David later became king of Israel and, through many triumphs and failures, he succeeded in becoming *"a man after His [God's] own heart"* (1 Samuel 13:14). Did you know that David was a mighty man of God, even though he made many mistakes and sinned against God? Yes, he was a sinner, just as we all are. The Bible says emphatically:

*For all have sinned and come short of the glory of God.*                              Romans 3:23, KJV

Remember that sin began in the Garden of Eden, and

**71**

every person born since then has sinned. The difference between David and some who don't know God is that David not only believed in God; he was also obedient to God, and he was repentant when he erred.

Repentance does not just mean saying we are sorry; it means turning and going the opposite way, away from our sinful life.

The story of David is just another example of how God uses the unlikely to fulfill His purposes. Another was his ancestor Ruth. Now let's take a look at how God used her in His plan. This will reveal more to us about God's ways and help us to find the answers to our common question, *Why, God?*.

Why, God?

# CHAPTER 8

# WHY KING DAVID AND JESUS WERE DESCENDED FROM A FOREIGNER

*Now it came to pass, in the days when the judges ruled, that there was a famine in the land. And a certain man of Bethlehem, Judah, went to dwell in the country of Moab, he and his wife and his two sons.*      Ruth 1:1

The book of Ruth is a story of one woman's persistence and faithfulness that placed her in a unique position in the lineage of King David and also of the Messiah, Jesus Christ. The story begins with these words from Ruth 1:1.

## NAOMI'S DESPERATE SITUATION

There was an Israelite by the name of Elimelech, and he had a wife named Naomi. This couple left Israel and moved to Moab, because there was a famine in the land. But Moab was a heathen country, one that did not worship the true and living God. It was a country inhabited by the descendants of Lot, whom we might remember from the story of Sodom. Moab, in fact, was named after the firstborn son of Lot (whose mother was one of Lot's own daughters). Ruth, too, was a citizen of this heathen country of Moab.

Naomi's husband, Elimelech, died and left Naomi with only her two sons. Both of her sons married wives from Moab. One of them was named Ruth, and the other was named Orpah. Then, both of these men also died, and that left Naomi with the responsibility to care, not only for herself, but also for Ruth and Orpah. In those days, it was a very serious thing for a woman to have to fend for herself, let alone for others.

When the economy of Moab suddenly got worse, Naomi found herself in a nearly impossible situation. Then she heard that God had blessed her homeland with food, so she and her daughters-in-law set out to return to the land of Judah.

## The Recommendation to Stay in Moab

On the way to Judah, Naomi had second thoughts. Maybe her daughters-in-law would not adapt to life in Israel. She told both Ruth and Orpah that it would be better for them to return to Moab so that they could have some kind of future in their own land, with their own people. Orpah agreed and returned to Moab, but Ruth answered her mother-in-law in this beautiful and poetic way:

*Entreat me not to leave you,*
*Or to turn back from following after you;*
*For wherever you go, I will go;*
*And wherever you lodge, I will lodge;*
*Your people shall be my people,*
*And your God, my God.*                    Ruth 1:16

Ruth was now so dedicated to Naomi that she was willing to leave her country and forsake her false gods to start a new life in a new country. She was also ready to serve the God of Israel.

## NAOMI'S WEALTHY KINSMAN

Naomi knew a wealthy kinsman of her husband whose name was Boaz. Since the harvest had begun, Naomi now told Ruth that she should go into the fields of Boaz and gather the corn leftover after the reapers had passed. In this way, she was hoping to find grace in the sight of Boaz.

That very day Boaz came to the field and saw Ruth gathering grains of corn that had been left by the reapers. He asked his servant who the woman was, and was told that she was the Moabite damsel who had come back with Naomi. Boaz talked to Ruth and told her she was welcome to reap in his fields. In fact, he told her not to reap from any other field except his. He also told her to stay with his female servants, and he instructed his men not to bother her.

Ruth bowed to Boaz and asked why she had found

grace in his sight. He responded that he had been told of her faithfulness to her mother-in-law. Faithfulness always pays off, and this is an important lesson for each of us today. Faithfulness to God and His purposes will increase His grace toward us. He loves us, even when we are unfaithful, but His grace is increased when we remain faithful.

Again, grace is God's unmerited favor, but it is also His goodwill and lovingkindness toward us. Boaz told Ruth :

*The Lord repay your work, and a full reward be given you by the Lord God of Israel, under whose wings you have come for refuge.* Ruth 2:12

In that moment, Boaz was pronouncing a blessing upon Ruth for trusting in God, and he was praying that God would give Ruth a *"full reward,"* or increased favor and grace. And, in fact, her trust in God did cause Ruth to be given increased favor, and so the prayer of Boaz was answered.

## GOING TO THE THRESHINGFLOOR

Because of Naomi's love for Ruth, she now told her daughter-in-law that Boaz was winnowing barley in his threshingfloor. He was a wealthy man, but he was sleeping at the threshingfloor to protect his harvest from thieves. Naomi told Ruth to wash, anoint, and dress herself, and then to go to the threshingfloor, but not to let Boaz know she was there. After Boaz had eaten dinner and had gone to bed, Ruth was to go and lie down near his feet. This was a very symbolic act. Ruth did as her mother-in-law had instructed.

At midnight Boaz was startled to find a woman at his feet. He asked her who she was, and she answered that she was his handmaiden Ruth. You can imagine why Boaz was startled by her presence. It was dark, and he may have thought that she was an intruder.

Ruth was not trying to be provocative, but in those days this act of lying at someone's feet was regarded as a sign of submission. There was a reason Ruth was to do this to Boaz. He was what was known in Bible days as a "kinsman redeemer," and this meant that Ruth actually had a right to expect Boaz to marry her and have children by her, to keep the name of Elimelech, his relative, alive.

## THE KINSMAN REDEEMER

A person known as a "kinsman redeemer" in Israel was called, in Hebrew, the *goel* or *ga'al*. The book of Deuteronomy speaks about the responsibility of the kinsman redeemer to carry on the family name by marrying a widow who had no children:

> *If brothers dwell together, and one of them dies and has no son, the widow of the dead man shall not be married to a stranger outside the family; her husband's brother shall go in to her, take her as his wife, and perform the duty of a husband's brother to her. And it shall be that the firstborn son which she bears will succeed to the*

*name of his dead brother, that his name may not be blotted out of Israel.*          Deuteronomy 25:5-6

So Boaz was required by Jewish law to marry Ruth, but, in actuality, he wanted to marry her. Still, even though he was a near kinsman to Elimelech, there was an even nearer kinsman who could have redeemed Ruth had he chosen to do so. So now Boaz would have to approach this man to find out if he would be willing to give up his rights to redeem Ruth. Boaz went to the gates of the city, where legal matters were settled, and there he sat down, hoping to see that other kinsman.

Sure enough, the man walked by, and Boaz was able to get his attention. This story can be found in Ruth chapter four. The outcome was that the man relinquished his rights to redeem Ruth, and Boaz then took Ruth to be his wife.

## OBED IS BORN

A son was born to this couple, and he was named *Obed,* which means "worshipping." The child was turned over to Naomi to nurse. Now wasn't that a turnaround for Naomi? She had previously said not to call her *"Naomi [pleasant],"* but to call her *"Mara [bitter]"* (Ruth 1:20). Now God blessed Naomi for her faithfulness, and the neighbor women actually said, *"There is a son born to Naomi"* (Ruth 4:17). How wonderful is our God? He is able to turn devastation into blessing.

Obed later had a son called Jesse, and, as we know,

King David was his son. David then had a descendant named Jesus! What a story! As we have noted, God chooses the foolish things of the world to confound the wise and the weak things of the world to confound the mighty. Ruth was a Moabite woman, who previously had served false gods, yet God used her in a mighty way to bring forth the Savior of the world, our Lord Jesus Christ.

## READ IT FOR YOURSELF

Let me encourage you to read the story of Ruth for yourself, in the light of how God uses ordinary people to perform extraordinary things for the sake of His Kingdom.

Why does God do the things He does? Because He alone has *the* plan for humanity, because He knows what is best for you and for me. God knows that without His help we would make a mess of our lives and of this world He has entrusted to us.

Remember, everything that God does is based on His love for us. What can stop God from loving us? Nothing! This is best described in Paul's letter to the Romans:

*Who shall separate us from the love of Christ? Shall tribulation, or distress, or persecution, or famine, or nakedness, or peril, or sword? As it is written:*

*"For Your sake we are killed all day long;*
*We are accounted as sheep for the slaughter."*

*Yet in all these things we are more than conquerors through Him who loved us. For I am persuaded that neither death nor life, nor angels nor principalities nor powers, nor things present nor things to come, nor height nor depth, nor any other created thing, shall be able to separate us from the love of God which is in Christ Jesus our Lord.* Romans 8:35-39

## God Wants YOU

God used many ordinary men and women throughout history to accomplish His plans and purposes. Some of these were noted in the Bible, and some were not. And God is still using ordinary men and women to accomplish great things for Him today. Many times God will use people in what looks like small acts. A kind word to a hurting person can change their life. A compassionate act of generosity has many times been the difference between someone giving up on life or going on with a fruitful future.

Throughout history there have been many kind, generous, compassionate individuals who have had profound impacts on the lives of others. Even now, every minute of every day, there are people who are blessing others and are making eternal deposits in Heaven. Do you want to be one of those people? Maybe you already are.

Remember that God desires people who love Him so much that they are willing to give up their rights in order to submit to His will.

## He Is Looking for the Available

God is always looking for the available. Are you available to Him? Are you ready and willing to be used by Him to touch the lives of others? If you are, then you are a candidate to become a servant of God, which is a very high calling indeed.

Some may say, "How can a lowly servant attain to a high calling"? Remember that God's ways are above our ways and His thoughts greater than our thoughts.

Again, Jesus told His disciples how to become great in the Kingdom of God:

*And He sat down, called the twelve, and said to them, "If anyone desires to be first, he shall be last of all and servant of all."*                    Mark 9:35

## Humble Yourself, as Jesus Did

Would you like to be more like Jesus? In writing to the Philippian church, Paul said:

*Let this mind be in you which was also in Christ Jesus, who, being in the form of God, did not consider it robbery to be equal with God, but made Himself of no reputation, taking the form of a bondservant, and coming in the likeness of men. And being found in appearance as a man, He humbled Himself and became obedient to the point of death, even the death of the cross.*                    Philippians 2:5-8

Because Jesus humbled Himself, the Father in Heaven *"highly exalted"* Him and gave Him a name *"which is above every name"*:

> *Therefore God also has highly exalted Him and given Him the name which is above every name, that at the name of Jesus every knee should bow, of those in heaven, and of those on earth, and of those under the earth, and that every tongue should confess that Jesus Christ is Lord, to the glory of God the Father.*
>
> Philippians 2:9-11

If Jesus, the Messiah, could humble Himself in the ways He did, are we not to humble ourselves in the same manner, by giving up our rights, in order to be a blessing to others? Ruth did it, and you can too.

Now, let's look at why we sometimes suffer financially. Our goal, as always, is to understand better the ways of God and see if we can find the answers to our common question, *Why, God?*.

# CHAPTER 9

# WHY WE SOMETIMES SUFFER FINANCIALLY

*Beloved, I pray that you may prosper in all things and be in health, just as your soul prospers.*    3 John 1:2

This is God's will for us, but what actually happens is often very different. And who's to blame for this fact? As we noted at the outset, it is normal for us to blame God for anything that doesn't seem to go right in our lives. It's wrong, and it's not a good thing to do, but we all do it. It's a human reaction to questions that we all have about the fairness of life. Let's use the example of a hardship most of us have encountered at one time or other in our lives—financial difficulties.

## YOU MAY WELL BE GOING THROUGH FINANCIAL DIFFICULTY

You may well be going through financial difficulty right now. Many are. When things are going well and finances are flowing, we're happy. But when things get tight financially, we become fearful, and we feel like we're under constant and tremendous pressure.

The truth is that many of the financial problems we face in life are our own fault, because of the poor decisions we have made. Still, we blame God.

Some might say, "Yes, but God could have kept me from making those wrong decisions." God can do anything, but always remember that He has given us all a free will. It's up to us what we do with all that God has given us.

## WE ARE ONLY STEWARDS

One of the first principles that we must understand is that we are only stewards of God's creation. The Bible says:

*The earth is the LORD's, and all its fullness,*
*The world and those who dwell therein.*   Psalm 24:1

In other words, God made the earth and everything in it, so it all belongs to Him. When He entrusts anything to us, we become stewards of what is rightfully His.

What kind of steward do you want to be? A good and faithful one, or a slothful and lazy one? Of course we all want to be good stewards of that which God has provided. But that requires wisdom, and it requires knowledge of what is pleasing to God.

## GOD'S THINKING ON MONEY
## IS CONTRARY TO OUR OWN

Since we are talking about the opposites of God, and we're still exploring His ways, let's look at God's plan for providing for our finances. It's a plan that is opposite of the way we usually think.

Let's look first at the normal way in which we earn and then utilize our finances. We go to work to earn an income, in order to provide for our needs. We put the money we earn into the bank so that we can write checks or use our debit cards to pay for the things we need, and if we have more then we need at any given time, we can invest it, in order to earn more money. It's pretty simple, isn't it? The way of the world is to provide for ourselves, but not for anyone else.

Now, it's a good thing to go to work to provide for yourself and your family. I'm not criticizing that. Paul the apostle said that if anyone would not work, they should not eat (see 2 Thessalonians 3:10), and all throughout the Bible God admonishes men not to be lazy. What's different about God's will for our finances is that He tells us to give Him the first ten percent, or what the Bible calls the *tithe*, of our income, before we spend the rest. Not everyone likes this idea of God's because, to our natural way of thinking, giving Him ten percent off the top seems exactly opposite to our way of achieving prosperity.

## The Importance of
## Paying Tithes and Giving Offerings

Way back in the book of Exodus, God told His people to bring the first of their fruits, or the firstfruits, of the land into His house. These firstfruits were to be an offering of thanks to Him. It was a sacrifice, a form of worship in recognition of our Creator.

Although this command was originally given to the Israelites, it still applies to God's people today, so we need to learn what the Bible teaches about finances.

For instance, the book of Proverbs tells us:

*Honor the Lord with your substance, and with the firstfruits of all your increase.* Proverbs 3:9

Ezekiel shows us that our firstfruits are holy (set apart or sanctified) to the Lord:

*And they shall not sell of it, neither exchange, nor alienate the firstfruits of the land: for it is holy unto the Lord.* Ezekiel 48:14

Leviticus shows us that the tithe is holy to the Lord:

*And all the tithe of the land, whether of the seed of the land, or of the fruit of the tree, is the Lord's: it is holy unto the Lord.* Leviticus 27:30

**86**

This same book also specifies that the tithe is a *"tenth"*:

*And concerning the tithe of the herd, or of the flock, even of whatsoever passeth under the rod, the tenth shall be holy unto the LORD.*      Leviticus 27:32

## THE TITHE AS SEED

The Bible also refers to the tithe as "seed" (Leviticus 27:32 and Deuteronomy 14:22). Any farmer knows that if his family eats all of their seed before it can be planted, there will be no future harvests. God gives us seed (or finances) and asks us to give back to Him just the first tenth, and that tenth becomes a seed toward our future harvests of financial blessings.

Isaiah teaches us:

*For as the rain comes down, and the snow from heaven,*
*And do not return there,*
*But water the earth,*
*And make it bring forth and bud,*
*That it may give seed to the sower*
*And bread to the eater, ...*      Isaiah 55:10

This shows that God has a plan to take care of our financial needs, and that plan includes giving to His Kingdom the first tenth of our income.

The Bible also encourages us to give offerings, as we are led by the Holy Spirit. Man's way is to hoard his finances, but God's way is to give.

## WHY BLAME GOD?

So why blame God when we suffer financially? If we live our lives according to His principals, we will be blessed. If we want to have things our own way, we will suffer the consequences, even though we may blame Him and/or others. Always remember that God is love, and all He wants to do is to show His love for you, by showing you His ways of living a joyful and fulfilled life.

God is never to blame for our problems. We are. Let's be honest about it. It's true that even when we are doing our best to submit to God, bad things still happen. That's when we just have to trust God and keep thanking and praising Him. That's true faith. Unfortunately, we will not have all the answers to our questions while we're here on this earth. I do believe, however, that God wants to be our Helper in this journey of life.

### OUR HELPER

God has provided His Holy Spirit for just that purpose. After Jesus was crucified, died, and was buried, He rose from the dead and appeared to some of the disciples. Before He ascended back to Heaven, He told them:

*And I will pray the Father, and He will give you another Helper, that He may abide with you forever—the Spirit of truth, whom the world cannot receive, because it neither sees Him nor knows Him; but you know Him, for He dwells with you and will be in you. I will not leave you orphans; I will come to you.*

John 14:16-18

So, why blame God when bad things happen? He loves you. He's on your side. He's not your enemy. He wants the very best for you. He's your Creator, and *"in Him we live, and move, and have our being"* (Acts 17:28).

You should come to realize that it's ridiculous to blame God for your problems. You may still have questions about why certain things happen in your life. That's perfectly normal.

As a matter of fact, it's a good thing to have questions about life, because this causes us to examine ourselves and our motives. I don't wish to open the proverbial "can of worms" here, but let's look at one of the most destructive motives any of us can have—selfishness.

## THE EVIL OF SELFISHNESS

Selfishness is totally opposite to how God operates, for it's the opposite of love. I often wonder, then, why I find myself being selfish, and I often wonder why humanity, in general, is selfish.

God is selfless. He gives, and He gives generously. He is love, and love gives and gives generously. As proof of this fact, one of the most powerful passages in the entire Bible, and one that we looked at in the very opening pages of the book, declares:

*For God so loved the world, that he gave his only begotten Son, that whosoever believeth in him should not perish, but have everlasting life. For God sent not his Son into the world to condemn the world: but that the world through him might be saved.*

John 3:16-17, KJV

If that's not selfless, then I don't know what is.

Our Father, His Son Jesus, and the Holy Spirit have the most beautiful home imaginable in Heaven. And yet the Father sent His only Son to earth to die for the sins of humanity, so that we would have everlasting life. That was selfless.

## WHAT IS SELFISHNESS?

What is selfishness? And what are some of the results of selfishness? Selfishness can take many forms: greed, pride, envy, lust, and simply just wanting our own way. Somehow we have come to think that we have a right to our way over the ways of others. If everyone else thought the same way, then we'd all be in trouble.

God's way is just the opposite. He wants us to give up our rights and prefer others before ourselves. He said:

*Be kindly affectioned one to another with brotherly love; in honor preferring one another.*

Romans 12:10, KJV

You may say, "But what about when someone does me wrong? Don't I have the right to retaliate?" Well, you can try to repay that person for their wrong, but who really gets hurt in the process? The truth is that, in any act of vengeance, the person who gets hurt most is the person who is repaying wrong with wrong. The Bible says:

> *Beloved, do not avenge yourselves, but rather give place to wrath; for it is written, "Vengeance is Mine, I will repay," says the Lord.*     Romans 12:19

## ANOTHER OPPOSITE

This leads us to another "opposite" of God. Human beings want vengeance when they are wronged, but God's ways is the way of forgiveness. Since God is love, forgiveness is part of His very nature. And if we desire to be like our Maker, then we, too, need to learn the power of forgiveness.

Unforgiveness is selfishness. The Bible says that if we cannot find it in our hearts to forgive others, then God will not be able to forgive us. Jesus Himself said:

> *For if you forgive men their trespasses, your heavenly Father will also forgive you. But if you do not forgive men their trespasses, neither will your Father forgive your trespasses.*     Matthew 6:14-15

**91**

Now, let's look at some concluding whys. Our goal, as always, is to learn more about God's ways and see if we can find the answers to our common question, *Why, God?*.

# CHAPTER 10

# SOME CONCLUDING WHYS

*I am the vine, you are the branches. He who abides in Me, and I in him, bears much fruit; for without Me you can do nothing.*                    John 15:5

Throughout the Bible you can read real stories of ordinary men, women, and even children who were used by God to fulfill His purposes. God's will is supreme, and He is the Creator. Therefore He has the right to rule this world in His own way.

Remember that His ways are high above our ways and that He knows best what is good for us. Therefore the conventional wisdom of man can never run the Universe. How very many times has man's way failed?

Again, Psalm 103:7 says that God *"made known His ways to Moses, His acts to the children of Israel."* Moses was God's leader at the time, and it was important for him to know how God operated. The people of Israel, as a whole, did not know God's *"ways,"* only His *"acts."* They just saw the results of His ways. If we can understand His ways, many of our whys will be answered.

## GOD'S WAYS IN BATTLE

One of the ways that God almost always does things "opposite" from man is in the area of battle. In the Old Testament, God sent His people into physical battles to drive out the heathen inhabitants from the Promised Land. When He wanted His people to go into battle, He told them to send the men of the tribe of Judah out first. Judah means "praise," so God was sending singers and musicians first into battle with "praise" to Him. How many military leaders would do that?

When the Israelites were obedient to go into battle in God's way, they were always victorious. For example, God delivered the great city of Jericho to His people by having them march around the city seven times. When, the priests had blown their trumpets and the people had shouted, the walls fell down flat.

In the time of the judges, God told Gideon how to do battle against the Midianites. First He told Gideon that he had too many men to defeat the Midianites. That seemed very strange because, in reality, the Midianites far out-numbered the men of Israel. Why, then, did God tell Gideon that he had too many men? God didn't want Israel to think that their own strength could save them. He told Gideon to tell the people who were fearful and afraid to leave the battlefield, and the result was that twenty-two thousand went home, and Gideon was left with only ten thousand fighting men.

Still, the Lord told Gideon that he had too many soldiers. He was to bring them to the water and test them. Those who lapped water with their tongue like a dog were to be set aside. Three hundred men drank in that way, and they were selected. The rest of the men bowed down on their knees to drink, and they were eliminated.

Now Gideon had only three hundred men, but God assured him that He would deliver the Midianites into his hand and save the nation by using those proven three hundred.

Next, God gave Gideon a plan for defeating the Midianites, and it, too, seemed strange. He was to divide the three hundred men into three groups and put a trumpet in every man's hand, but also an empty pitcher and a lamp inside of that pitcher. Gideon told the men to look at him and do what he did. He said:

> *When I blow the trumpet, I and all who are with me, then you also blow the trumpets on every side OF the whole camp, and say, "The sword of the LORD and of Gideon!"*  Judges 7:18

So, all the men blew their trumpets, broke their pitchers, and held up their lamps. The lamps were in their left hands, and the trumpets were in their right. When they blew the trumpets and cried out those prescribed words: *"the sword of the LORD and of Gideon,"* the Midianites suddenly jumped up and, confused, began to run in all directions, crying out in fear. Then they turned and fled for their lives.

This all happened in the middle of the night. Can you imagine the fear they felt at being awakened by a flash of light in the dark and the sound of trumpets and shouting and the crashing sound of the pots? God knew just how to deal with these enemies. How easily Gideon and his three hundred men destroyed the Midianites with their swords! Wow, what a story of victory!

We don't know exactly how many of the enemy soldiers there had been, but the Bible says that they were *"as grasshoppers for multitude"* (Judges 6:5 and 7:12). Our God can give us victory over a multitude, if we will just obey Him. His ways are always best.

## JESUS SAID IT WELL

Over and over again, God shows us, His people, that without Him, we are nothing, but, with Him, we can do all things. Jesus said it well:

*I am the vine, ye are the branches: he that abideth in me, and I in him, the same bringeth forth much fruit: for without me you can do nothing.* John 15:5, JKV

Just as we can do nothing of any eternal or spiritual value without God, Jesus said (in Luke 1:37) *"for with God nothing shall be impossible"* (KJV). He said (in Matthew 19:26 and Mark 10:27) that *"with God all things are possible"* (KJV). In Matthew 21:22, He said that if we believed we would receive all the things we ask for in prayer. He said (in Mark 9:23) that *"all things are possible to him that believeth"* (KJV). That means *"all things."*

## ANOTHER REASON

Another reason that God does things differently than we would is that He wants us to totally trust Him in every part of our lives. He wants us to acknowledge Him as our Creator and as our Lord. He wants us to love Him as a Father who is looking out for our best interests. He wants us to put aside our pride and to humbly accept His help in everything that we do. God wants us to recognize and realize that He is almighty and well able to deliver us from every adverse situation.

Under the Old Covenant, before Jesus came and established the New Covenant (by shedding His blood at His death and rising from the dead), the Israelites fought their enemies with physical force. Now, in this New Covenant period. we fight the spiritual enemies of our souls, and we must do it with spiritual weapons. The Bible says:

*For the weapons of our warfare are not carnal but mighty in God for pulling down strongholds.*
2 Corinthians 10:4

Before we establish a personal relationship with Jesus Christ, we cannot understand how we could possibly fight a battle without physical weapons. We have enemies, but they are not flesh and blood; they are the spiritual enemies of our souls. Satan is the leader of those enemies. He is an evil spirit who was cast out of Heaven along with one-third of the angels who followed him.

The sin that caused the downfall of Satan and his angels was pride. Of pride, the Bible says:

*Pride goes before destruction, and a haughty spirit before a fall.*                    Proverbs 16:18

God hates pride because pride says: "I can do it by myself; I don't need God." Pride is an utter rejection of our Creator. God's way for you to overcome your spiritual enemies is for you to use spiritual weapons and to put on spiritual armor.

In writing to the Ephesians, Paul spoke of the armor of God and the weapons of our warfare (see Ephesians 6:10-18). It is important to know God's ways because we are human, and we make mistakes. God knows us wall, and He wants to help us to be victorious in this life.

## GOD'S IDEAS ABOUT THE IMPORTANCE OF PRAYER

Another way that God operates differently than us is in the area of prayer. Man's way of changing his situation is to do things on his own. Common sense says that if you want something done, do it yourself. Common sense says to pull yourself up by your bootstraps. Pride and arrogance say, "I don't need anyone's help; I can do it myself." God's way says, *"I can do all things through Christ which strengthens me"* (Philippians 4:13). God's way says that His Holy Spirit is our Helper. God's way says that, with Him, *"nothing shall be impossible."*

But how do we get the help we need from God? Prayer is the key! James wrote to the early Church:

> *Is any among you afflicted? let him pray. Is any merry? Let him sing psalms. Is any sick among you? Let him call for the elders of the church; and let them pray over him, anointing him with oil in the name of the Lord: and the prayer of faith shall save the sick, and the Lord shall raise him up; and if he hath committed sins, they shall be forgiven him.*
>
> *Confess your faults one to another, and pray one for another, that ye may be healed. The effectual fervent prayer of a righteous man availeth much.*
>
> *Elijah was a man subject to like passions as we are, and he prayed earnestly that it might not rain: and it rained not on the earth by the space of three years and six months. And he prayed again, and the heaven gave rain, and the earth brought forth her fruit.*
>
> James 5:13-18, KJV

God wants us to pray and to pray with faith. In other words, He wants us to ask for His help and to believe that He *will* help us.

He also wants us to pray fervently. Let's look again at part of verse 16. It says *"the effectual fervent prayer of a righteous man availeth much."* The New Testament of the Bible was written in the Greek language and later translated into English. Sometimes, in the translation, we lose part of the real meaning.

This word *effectual,* in the Greek, means "to be active or efficient." The word *fervent* means "heat, zeal, or ardor." The word *availeth* means "might or to prevail." If you substitute these words in the scripture, to better understand it, you may read it like this: "The active, efficient, hot and zealous prayer of a righteous person has might and will prevail."

This verse is trying to stress the importance of praying in a manner that is intense. In other words, if we are righteous, because of our faith in Jesus Christ, then we should pray with active, efficient, hot, and zealous faith, in order for our prayers to have might and to prevail over the negative attacks of the enemy.

## PRAY IN FAITH

God wants us to pray in faith, so that we actually see the answers to our prayers before they happen. Jesus said:

*If you have faith as a mustard seed, you shall say to this mountain, "Move from here to there," and it will move; and nothing will be impossible for you.*

Matthew 17:20

The mustard seed is one of the smallest seeds. What Jesus was saying is that even if you have just a little faith (the size of a mustard seed), you can receive unimaginable answers to your prayers.

All throughout the Bible, prayer is mentioned by God and the prophets as essential to receiving the help of our Creator. Even when we ask God "Why?" it is a prayer. Prayer is any communication with God.

## COMMUNICATION IS TWO WAY

Communication is two way. We ask God questions, and He answers. We talk to God, and He talks to us. Let me encourage you to talk to Him, and also to listen for His voice in reply. Sometimes we are so busy and tense that we need to settle ourselves down, be still, and listen for His voice.

At one point, the prophet Elijah was in great distress and needed to hear from God. God told him to go stand upon a mountain before the Lord. We read:

> *And behold, the* LORD *passed by, and a great and strong wind tore into the mountains and broke the rocks in pieces before the* LORD, *but the* LORD *was not in the wind; and after the wind an earthquake, but the* LORD *was not in the earthquake; and after the earthquake a fire, but the* LORD *was not in the fire; and after the fire a still small voice. So it was, when Elijah heard it, that he wrapped his face in his mantle and went out and stood in the entrance of the cave. Suddenly a voice came to him, and said, "What are you doing here, Elijah?"*
>
> 1 Kings 19:11-13

**101**

God answered Elijah in a *"still small voice."* Our God is mighty enough to bring winds and earthquakes and fires, but He wants us to draw near enough to Him to hear His faintest whisper.

James tells us:

*Draw near to God and He will draw near to you.*

James 4:8

When we are "born again" of the Holy Spirit by our faith in Jesus Christ, we are adopted as sons and daughters of the most high God. We become His children and, thus, have access to Him whenever we need or want. His desire is that we get close enough to Him that we can hear His words of wisdom for us.

Remember that God wants the best for you. He's not out to punish you, but to promote you. He loves you so much that He gave His one and only Son to die for your sins, in order to save you from eternal damnation. God does not want His children to die and go to Hell. He wants us to be with Him forever in Heaven.

## WHO KNOWS?

Who knows what Hell is really like? You can only speculate about how bad it is. We do know that it is a place of darkness and fire and brimstone. It is a place of eternal separation from God and loved ones who have gone to Heaven. Jesus gave us an idea of Hell in the story of Lazarus:

*There was a certain rich man who was clothed in purple and fine linen and fared sumptuously every day. But there was a certain beggar named Lazarus, full of sores, who was laid at his gate, desiring to be fed with the crumbs which fell from the rich man's table. Moreover the dogs came and licked his sores. So it was that the beggar died, and was carried by the angels to Abraham's bosom. The rich man also died and was buried. And being in torments in Hades, he lifted up his eyes and saw Abraham afar off, and Lazarus in his bosom.*

*Then he cried and said, "Father Abraham, have mercy on me, and send Lazarus that he may dip the tip of his finger in water and cool my tongue; for I am tormented in this flame."*

*But Abraham said, "Son, remember that in your lifetime you received your good things, and likewise Lazarus evil things; but now he is comforted and you are tormented. And besides all this, between us and you there is a great gulf fixed, so that those who want to pass from here to you cannot, nor can those from there pass to us."*

*"Then he said, 'I beg you therefore, father, that you would send him to my father's house, for I have five brothers, that he may testify to them, lest they also come to this place of torment."*

*Abraham said to him, "They have Moses and the prophets; let them hear them."*

*And he said, "No, father Abraham; but if one goes
to them from the dead, they will repent."
But he said to him, "If they do not hear Moses
and the prophets, neither will they be persuaded
though one rise from the dead."* Luke 16:19-31

Let me tell you, my friend, One did rise from
the dead over two thousand years ago. His name is
Jesus Christ, and He is the Son of the living God! He
died for your sins, and He died for mine. He was
buried for three days, and on the third day He was
raised from the dead by the power of the Holy Spirit
and returned to be with His Father in Heaven.

## What Is Jesus Doing
## at the Father's Right Hand?

Jesus is still sitting at the right hand of the Father, and there He is praying for you. What is He
praying? Only the Father knows, but I can speculate
that Jesus is praying that you will believe that the
Father sent Him to this earth in the form of human
flesh, to die for your sins, so that you can have everlasting life. I think He is praying that you will
accept Him as Lord of your life. I think that He is
praying that you will turn from your own way of
running your life and ask Him to help you to live
your life.

We're nearing the end of our journey together. Now, in a final chapter, we need to look at the all important subject of why we need a Savior. In doing so, let us seek to understand better the ways of God and find the answers to our common question, Why, God?.

# CHAPTER 11

# WHY WE NEED A SAVIOR

*All have sinned, and come short of the glory of God.*
                                        Romans 3:23

*The soul who sins shall die.*          Ezekiel 18:20

Earlier in this book we looked at the sin of Adam and Eve. Because of their disobedience, they brought sin into the world. The Bible declares: *"The soul who sins shall die."* And Paul, the great apostle, wrote to the Romans, *"All have sinned, and come short of the glory of God."* Sin causes us to miss the mark, or goal, of eternity with God in Heaven.

## MAN IS SINFUL

Ever since the first sin of Adam and Eve, people have been sinning against their Creator. His own people Israel and even His very leaders sinned against Him repeatedly.

This is serious, for the Bible shows that *"the wages of sin is death"*:

*For the wages of sin is death; but the gift of God is eternal life through Jesus Christ our Lord.*

Romans 6:23

If all people from the beginning of time have sinned, and the wages of sin is death, then how is there any hope for the salvation of mankind?

After the sin of Adam and Eve, God gave His people a means of covering their past sins. He told them to offer sacrifices of animals, and that would give them a temporary reprieve for their sins. The writer of the Hebrews declared:

*Without shedding of blood there is no remission.*

Hebrews 9:22

In other words, blood had to be shed to obtain forgiveness, or pardon, from sins. Some innocent sacrifice had to die to atone for the sins of the guilty party. The sinner remained sinful and continued sinning, but their past transgressions were covered.

## THE SINLESS FOR THE SINFUL

God gave His people very specific instructions about how to offer their sacrifices for sin. One prerequisite was that the animals sacrifices had to be free from blemishes. They had to be the best animals that were available. They had to be spotless. They had to be innocent and pure. This innocence and purity was just the opposite from the people offering the sacrifices, since they were sinners. Innocent animals had to give their lives to die for the sins of guilty people. Looking back on it now, this seems so unfair.

And yet this killing of innocent animals went on for many hundreds of years in Old Testament history, because the people continually sinned. This proves that we all need a savior. We are all sinners, and the wages of sin is death, so unless we find a savior, we are headed for eternal damnation. We need someone to take our place and die for our sins. Again, this seems unfair, just as it was unfair for innocent animals to take the place of the guilty Israelites.

When Jesus came to this earth, as God in the flesh, He came to be the Savior we all need. Why would God, the Father, send His only Son to a sinful, disobedient people who did not deserve to be saved? How many times have we been disobedient and rebellious to God? Do we deserve to be saved from spiritual death and Hell? No! And yet, thank God that we don't have to receive the just penalty for our sin. Jesus came to offer His spotless, innocent body to be crucified for us, and to shed His precious blood for you and me—all because of His love.

In the Introduction to this book, I quoted John 3:16. Let's look at it one more time:

*For God so loved the world, that he gave his only begotten Son, that whosoever believeth in him should not perish, but have everlasting life: for God sent not his Son into the world to condemn the world; but that the world through him might be saved.*

John 3:16-17, KJV

Remember those spotless animals that were sacrificed for the sins of the Israelites? The Scriptures refer to Jesus as a spotless lamb. For instance, when John the Baptist began his ministry and was baptizing people with water in the Jordan river, he saw Jesus coming to him one day and said to the crowd:

*Behold! The Lamb of God who takes away the sin of the world!*                    John 1:29

John also said that he saw the Holy Spirit descending from Heaven like a dove upon Jesus and remaining upon Him. This caused him to say:

*This is the Son of God.*                    John 1:34

The very next day John and two of his disciples saw Jesus, and he again said:

*Behold the Lamb of God!*                    John 1:36

Hundreds of years before, Isaiah had prophesied concerning Jesus:

*He was oppressed and He was afflicted,*
*Yet He opened not His mouth;*
*He was led as a lamb to the slaughter,*
*And as a sheep before its shearers is silent,*
*So He opened not His mouth.*　　　　　Isaiah 53:7

The book of Acts records the story of Philip reading from these Scriptures to an Ethiopian eunuch:

*He was led as a sheep to the slaughter;*
*And as a lamb before its shearer is silent,*
*So He opened not His mouth.*　　　　　Acts 8:32

When Jesus was betrayed by Judas, He was brought before the high priest, a man named Caiaphas. Jesus had just raised His good friend Lazarus from the dead, and some of the Jews went to the Pharisees and told them what He had done. This is what ensued:

*Then the chief priests and the Pharisees gathered a*
*council and said, "What shall we do? For this Man*
*works many signs. If we let Him alone like this, every-*
*one will believe in Him, and the Romans will come and*
*take away both our place and nation."*
*And one of them, Caiaphas, being high priest that year,*
*said to them, "You know nothing at all, nor do you*
*consider that it is expedient for us that one man should*
*die for the people, and not that the whole nation should*
*perish." Now this he did not say on his own author-*
*ity; but being high priest that year he prophesied that*

**111**

*Jesus would die for the nation, and not for that nation only, but also that He would gather together in one the children of God who were scattered abroad.*
*Then, from that day on, they plotted to put Him to death.*                          John 11:47-53

After Caiaphas had questioned Jesus about His disciples and His doctrine, he sent Him to Pontius Pilate, who was then Governor of Judea. Jesus was then questioned by Pilate and the chief priests and elders, and He declined to answer them, thus fulfilling the scriptures, which had been previously written in Isaiah 53:7, that the Messiah would be led as a lamb to the slaughter, and yet He would not open His mouth. In the days ahead, Jesus was pronounced innocent by many, including Judas himself, when he told the chief priests and elders:

*I have sinned by betraying innocent blood.*
                                        Matthew 27:4

The wife of Pilate warned him:

*Have nothing to do with that just Man, for I have suffered many things today in a dream because of Him.*
                                        Matthew 27:19

Pilate did not want to crucify Jesus, and he said to the people:

*What evil has he done?*                 Matthew 27:23

When they would not be persuaded, he then washed his hands of the matter, saying to them:

*I am innocent of the blood of this just Person. You see to it.*                                    Matthew 27:24

Luke quoted Pilate as saying, *"I find no fault in this Man"* (Luke 23:4). The point is that Jesus is the pure and innocent Lamb of God! Peter later wrote to the Church:

*You were not redeemed with corruptible things, like silver or gold, from your aimless conduct received by tradition from your fathers, but with the precious blood of Christ, as of a lamb without blemish and without spot.*                                    1 Peter 1:18-19

Remember, again, that without the shedding of blood there is no forgiveness of sins, but Jesus shed His blood for us.

## THE POWER OF JESUS' BLOOD

In chapters 9 and 10 of the book of Hebrews, there is an explanation of the importance of Jesus shedding His blood for our salvation. After He died, was buried, and resurrected, He took His own blood to Heaven and placed it on the Mercy Seat, on top of the Ark of the Covenant. This indicated that it was no longer necessary for the people to offer the blood of lambs or bullocks to cover their sins, since Jesus had died, once and for all, for the complete forgiveness of our sins. Hebrews then states:

> *But Christ came as High Priest of the good things to come, with the greater and more perfect tabernacle not made with hands, that is, not of this creation. Not with the blood of goats and calves, but with His own blood He entered the Most Holy Place once for all, having obtained eternal redemption.* Hebrews 9:11-12

There is much more that could be said about the benefits of the precious blood of Jesus and of the establishment and ratification of the New Covenant by Christ, but that's for another book! The point we need to make here is that we need a savior because, without Christ, we are like sheep without a shepherd. We have lived our lives our own way, separate from God.

## I Know These Things Are True

Until we have a personal relationship with Jesus, we are empty, and our lives have no meaning. We try to fulfill ourselves with alcohol, drugs, illicit sex, and many other things, but they all bring us only a temporary high. It seems that we are always seeking some new thrill to satisfy the deepest needs in our lives, and these needs are never met. We always find ourselves empty and depressed. There is always a hole in our heart, which we try, in vain, to fill.

I know these things are true because I lived them

myself. When I heard the Gospel (the Good News) of Christ, and I accepted Him into my heart, my whole life changed. Suddenly my life had meaning. I realized that I was a sinner on the way to Hell, I saw that I deserved to go to Hell because of my sin and disobedience, and I repented of my sin and asked Jesus to forgive me and to save me. And He did!

Immediately, when I would read the Bible, I found that my eyes were opened, and I understood the Scriptures. I began to go to church. I began to sing about the goodness and greatness of God. My life was not perfect, but I had a new joy in my soul. I felt the forgiveness of God, I felt the presence of God, I experienced the mercy of God, and I felt the love of God for me.

As I went to church on a regular basis, I was taught the Word of God. I was taught the importance of praising and worshipping God. I learned a lot by personal reading and study of the Bible. I learned how to communicate with God through prayer. Now, after more than thirty years of serving Christ, I'm still not perfect, but I know that I am forgiven and that God loves me and He has my best interests at heart. I still ask God *why* sometimes, but I want to know His ways better, so I won't have to ask as often.

## CAN YOU RELATE?

Let me ask you, dear reader: can you relate to my story? Where are you in regard to eternity? Have you ever sinned, and do you feel sorry for your sins? Do you feel that God just wants to punish you? Do you think that God hates you? These are normal feelings, and God understands how you feel. The prophet Isaiah, speaking of Jesus, the Messiah, said:

*He is despised and rejected by men,*
*A Man of sorrows and acquainted with grief.*
*And we hid, as it were, our faces from Him;*
*He was despised, and we did not esteem Him.*

Isaiah 53:3

## HE IS OUR GREAT HIGH PRIEST

Jesus is our high priest, and Hebrews declares:

*For we do not have a High Priest who cannot sympathize with our weaknesses, but was in all points tempted as we are, yet without sin.*     Hebrews 4:15

Since God is the Creator of all, including you and me, don't you think He knows how we feel? We are made in His very image. He wants us to look like He looks, not only on the outside, but in our hearts, as well.

So what does God look like? It will take the rest of our lives to find out. We know that He is love. He is also mercy. He is kind. He is generous. He is beautiful. He is our Helper. He's our Deliverer. He's our Redeemer. He's the Mighty God, the Everlasting Father, the Prince of Peace. He's our Healer. He's our help in times of trouble.

God is all powerful. He's all knowing. He is our all in

**116**

all. God is awesome! God gives, and He wants you and I to be givers as well. He wants us to follow in His footsteps, just as a child follows their parents.

How can we give to others? We can give our time, our love, our finances, our godly counsel, our encouragement, and our prayers. Jesus told of a king who spoke to a godly people and said:

*For I was hungry and you gave Me food; I was thirsty and you gave Me drink; I was a stranger and you took Me in; I was naked and you clothed Me; I was sick and you visited Me; I was in prison and you came to Me.*
Matthew 25:35-36

They were surprised by this and asked Him:

*Lord, when did we see You hungry and feed You, or thirsty and give You drink? 38 When did we see You a stranger and take You in, or naked and clothe You? 39 Or when did we see You sick, or in prison, and come to You?*
Matthew 25:37-39

The answer they received should speak to us all:

*Assuredly, I say to you, inasmuch as you did it to one of the least of these My brethren, you did it to Me.*
Matthew 25:40

So when we give to others, we are actually giving to God!

You may say, "I know that others can be good and loving, but I don't know how I can." In our own ability, we cannot be good. We are only able to be godly when we accept God's free gift of salvation through His Son Jesus Christ.

## The Good News of the Gospel

The word *gospel* means "good news," and the good news is that even though we are sinners and deserve death, Jesus made a way for us to have everlasting life! He died in *our* place. When He willingly went to the cross, more than two thousand years ago now, He took our sin upon His own body and bore it to the grave. The Bible shows us:

> *Christ has redeemed us from the curse of the law, having become a curse for us (for it is written, "Cursed is everyone who hangs on a tree"), that the blessing of Abraham might come upon the Gentiles in Christ Jesus, that we might receive the promise of the Spirit through faith.*　　　　Galatians 3:13-14

Jesus took the curse of our sin (which is spiritual death) on His body on the tree of Calvary. He died there, and was then buried and descended into Hell itself. There He left our sin. Also, while He was there, He stripped Satan of the keys of death, Hell, and the grave. And three days later He arose from the dead, to ascend to be with the Father in Heaven.

So, Jesus died for our sins. He took the penalty for our sins upon Himself, because of His love for us. We are His children, and He wants us to be with Him and the Father and the Holy Spirit in the everlasting Kingdom of God.

Some insist that there are many paths to God, but Jesus said:

*I am the way, the truth, and the life. No one comes to the Father except through Me.*                John 14:6

## Jesus Fulfilled the Prophecies of the Old Testament

Jesus, the Messiah, is the only one who died for your sins. He fulfilled the countless prophecies of the Old Testament concerning the Messiah. For instance, the Scriptures foretold that the Messiah would be born of a virgin in the small town of Bethlehem. They foretold that He would be called out of Egypt. They said that He would be called a Nazarene. Here, compliments of *How to Find God in the New Testament* (Carol Stream, Illinois, Tyndale House Publishers: 1996) are some of those amazing prophecies, showing their Old Testament reference and their New Testament fulfillment:

| The Prophecy | The Old Testament Reference | The New Testament Fulfillment |
| --- | --- | --- |
| Messiah was to be born in Bethlehem | Micah 5:2 | Matthew 2:1-6 Luke 2:1-20 |
| Messiah was to be born of a virgin | Isaiah 7:14 | Matthew 1:18-25 Luke 1:26-38 |

| The Prophecy | The Old Testament Reference | The New Testament Fulfillment |
|---|---|---|
| Messiah was to be a prophet, like Moses | Deuteronomy 18:15 and 18-19 | John 7:40 |
| Messiah was to enter Jerusalem in triumph | Zechariah 9:9 | Matthew 21:1-9 John 12:12-16 |
| Messiah was to be rejected by His own people | Isaiah 53:1-3 Psalm 118:22 | Matthew 26:3-4 John 12:37-43 Acts 4:1-12 |
| Messiah was to be betrayed by one of His followers | Psalm 41:9 | Matthew 26:14-16 & 47-50 Luke 23:16 & 47-48 |
| Messiah was to be tried and condemned | Isaiah 53:8 | Luke 23:1-25 Matthew 27:1-2 |
| Messiah was to be silent before His accusers | Isaiah 53:7 | Matthew 26:62-63 & 27:12-14 Mark 15:3-5 Luke 23:8-10 |
| Messiah was to be mocked and taunted | Psalm 22:7-8 | Matthew 27:39-44 Luke 23:11 & 35-36 |
| Messiah was to die by crucifixion | Psalm 22:14 & 16-17 | Matthew 27:31 Mark 15:20 & 25 |
| Messiah was to suffer with criminals and pray for His enemies | Isaiah 53:12 | Matthew 27:38 Mark 15:27-28 Luke 23:32-34 |
| Messiah was to be given vinegar and gall | Psalm 69:21 | Matthew 27:34 John 19:28-30 |
| Others were to cast lots for Messiah's garments | Psalm 22:18 | Matthew 27:35 John 19:23-24 |
| Messiah's bones were not to be broken | Exodus 12:46 | John 19:31-36 |
| Messiah was to die as a sacrifice for sin | Isaiah 53:5-6, 8 and 10-12 | John 1:29 & 11:49-52 Acts 10:43 & 13:38-39 |

| THE PROPHECY | THE OLD TESTAMENT REFERENCE | THE NEW TESTAMENT FULFILLMENT |
|---|---|---|
| Messiah was to be raised from the dead | Psalm 16:10 | Matthew 28:1-10<br>Mark 16:1-8<br>Luke 24:1-12<br>John 20:1-9<br>Acts 2:22-32 |
| Messiah is now at the Father's right hand | Psalm 110:1 | Mark 16:19<br>Luke 24:50-51 |

These are just a few examples of the prophecies that Jesus fulfilled. Some say that Elijah must come before the Messiah comes. Malachi declared:

*Behold, I will send you Elijah the prophet*
*Before the coming of the great and dreadful day of the*
*LORD.*                                            Malachi 4:5

Some don't believe that Jesus is the Messiah, but Jesus Himself said:

*And from the days of John the Baptist until now the*
*kingdom of heaven suffers violence, and the violent take*
*it by force. For all the prophets and the law prophesied*
*until John. And if you are willing to receive it, he is*
*Elijah who is to come. He who has ears to hear, let him*
*hear!*                                        Matthew 11:12-15

Jesus was saying that Elijah did come again to pave the way for the coming of the Messiah. John the Baptist came in the spirit of Elijah. He came proclaiming the coming of the Kingdom of God.

## Which Other God Can Save You?

Which other god can save you? Which of the many false gods died for your sin? Many graves contain the bones of false gods. They died.

How many false gods have fulfilled every prophecy concerning the Messiah? None! There is only one God, and He has sent His only begotten Son to die for your sins. There is only one God, and His Son's bones cannot be found in any grave, because He was raised from the dead, and He ascended into Heaven. There is only one God, and His Son fulfilled every prophecy about the Messiah. He is the one and only true and living God, and He is King of kings and Lord of lords.

Moses said:

*Hear, O Israel: The Lord our God, the Lord is one! You shall love the Lord your God with all your heart, with all your soul, and with all your strength.*

*Deuteronomy 6:4-5*

Jeremiah said:

*But the Lord is the true God; He is the living God and the everlasting King. At His wrath the earth will tremble,*

*And the nations will not be able to endure His indignation.* Jeremiah 10:10

Our great God will come one day to judge the living and the dead. His wrath will be poured out upon unrepentant sinners. His fury will be unleashed on the rebellious, those who said no to His free gift of salvation through Jesus Christ, the Messiah. To those who accept what Jesus did for them, He will grant everlasting life. God wants all of us to be saved, for He loves every one of us. However, He knows that not everyone will believe in Him.

## WHAT MUST WE DO TO BE SAVED?

So what must we do to be saved? There is a true story in the book of Acts concerning the imprisonment of the apostle Paul and his companion Silas. At midnight, they were praying and singing praises to God, and the other prisoners overheard them. Then something wonderful happened:

*Suddenly there was a great earthquake, so that the foundations of the prison were shaken; and immediately all the doors were opened and everyone's chains were loosed. And the keeper of the prison, awaking from sleep and seeing the prison doors open, supposing the prisoners had fled, drew his sword and was about to kill himself. But Paul called with a loud voice, saying, "Do yourself no harm, for we are all here."*

*Then he called for a light, ran in, and fell down trembling before Paul and Silas. And he brought them out and said, "Sirs, what must I do to be saved?"*
*So they said, "Believe on the Lord Jesus Christ, and you will be saved, you and your household." Then they spoke the word of the Lord to him and to all who were in his house. And he took them the same hour of the night and washed their stripes. And immediately he and all his family were baptized.*      Acts 16:26-33

In a few short words, Paul gave this prison keeper the formula for salvation, and he was saved that very night. Paul wrote to the Romans:

*That if you confess with your mouth the Lord Jesus and believe in your heart that God has raised Him from the dead, you will be saved. For with the heart one believes unto righteousness, and with the mouth confession is made unto salvation.*      Romans 10:9-10

God requires only that we believe with our hearts and then confess with our mouths that Jesus is Lord.

## REPENTANCE IS PART OF THE PICTURE

Repentance is also part of the picture:

*Then Peter said to them, "Repent, and let every one of you be baptized in the name of Jesus Christ for the remission of sins; and you shall receive the gift of the Holy Spirit."*       Acts 2:38

*Repent therefore and be converted, that your sins may be blotted out, so that times of refreshing may come from the presence of the Lord, and that He may send Jesus Christ, who was preached to you before,.*

Acts 3:19-20

Repent today, and God will answer your prayer.

## DO YOU NEED A REFRESHING?

Do you, perhaps, need a refreshing from the presence of the Lord? Do you want freedom from the guilt of sin? How would it feel to be able to enter into the presence of God with no embarrassment or shame? Well, you can have that. You can have joy unspeakable and full of glory. You can feel the warmth, consolation, and love of God. He wants you to come into His presence with thanksgiving and praise. He wants you to call upon Him in every season of your life. He is waiting for you. He will not force His will upon you.

## PRAY THIS PRAYER

If you want this kind of forgiveness, freedom from the guilt of sin, and the knowledge that when you die, you will be with God forever, let me encourage you to pray this simple prayer of faith in Jesus Christ:

God,

I acknowledge that I am a sinner. I have lived my life my own way, separate from You. I ask You to forgive me of all of my sins. Today, I want to make a change in my life. I now believe, with all my heart, that You sent Jesus Christ to be my Savior and to die for my sins. I believe that Jesus Christ is Your Son and that He died, was buried, and was resurrected from the dead. I also confess that I accept Jesus Christ as my Lord and Savior. I invite You now into my heart, Lord Jesus, and thank You for saving me today!                              AMEN!

## WELCOME TO THE BODY OF CHRIST

If you prayed this prayer with sincerity, I believe you are now saved. The Bible declares:

*There is joy in the presence of the angels of God over one sinner who repents.*                    Luke 15:10

So, welcome to the Body of Christ. God has great plans for you. Let me encourage you to find and regularly attend a Bible-believing church. Let me encourage you to start reading and studying the Bible and to talk to your Father every day through prayer. Let me encourage you to sing praises and worship to God daily and to thank Him for His marvelous works! If you do these things, you will prosper spiritually.

Hopefully this book has helped you to understand God's ways a little better, and when you have "whys" in the future, you will know that God wants to answer you, because He loves you with all of His heart!

*Dear Reader,*

*If this book has been a blessing to you, you wish to share a testimony with me, or you want to give your life to Christ, please contact me by email: skblyt@cox.net.*

*Skip Blythe*